DIGITAL AFRICA

DIGITAL AFRICA

Investing in Africa's
Most Untapped Source

JESPER DRESCHER

Copyright © 2020 Jesper Drescher
All rights reserved. No part of this book may be used or reproduced in any manner whatsoever without prior written consent of the authors, except as provided by the United States of America copyright law.

Published by Best Seller Publishing®, Pasadena, CA
Best Seller Publishing® is a registered trademark
Printed in the United States of America.
ISBN 978-87-972676-0-8

This publication is designed to provide accurate and authoritative information with regard to the subject matter covered. It is sold with the understanding that the publisher is not engaged in rendering legal, accounting, or other professional advice. If legal advice or other expert assistance is required, the services of a competent professional should be sought. The opinions expressed by the authors in this book are not endorsed by Best Seller Publishing® and are the sole responsibility of the author rendering the opinion.

For more information, please write:
Best Seller Publishing®
253 N. San Gabriel Blvd, Unit B
Pasadena, CA 91107
or call 1(626) 765 9750
Visit us online at: www.BestSellerPublishing.org

Table of Contents

Preface 1

Introduction: Is Sub-Saharan Africa the Next China? 3

Chapter One: The African Entrepreneurial Opportunity 19

Chapter Two: To Invest for Impact or for Growth? 31

Chapter Three: Why Digitalization is the Biggest Lever in Developing Sub-Saharan Africa..45

Chapter Four: The Tech Investment Eco-System in Sub-Saharan Africa..61

Chapter Five: Building Successful Businesses in Sub-Saharan Africa: Innovative Ideas and Business Models 81

Chapter Six: Recruiting People and Building Partnerships in African Start-Ups..117

Chapter Seven: The Future of Sub-Saharan Africa— and Why It's Not Here Now...143

Conclusion—Digitalizing Africa...155

Preface

My main reason for writing this book is to help a continent that I love and believe in deeply. I want to use the knowledge that I've acquired building businesses in Africa over the last few years to help investors and local entrepreneurs to lower their risks, know what to expect, and build the successful technology firms that the region needs.

Many people talk about investing in Africa, but few people have the guts to do it. It's a difficult environment for investors, filled with unknown hazards and unexpected challenges. From reviewing business ideas through talent recruitment, funding, and adjusting to the continent's market conditions, Africa is never short of surprises.

It's also a wonderful place, filled with amazing, creative, hardworking people who want nothing more than to create new businesses, build their careers, deliver services and products, and move their countries and their families forward to a new and more prosperous future.

In his book, *Factfulness*, statistician Hans Rosling explains why the world is becoming a better, wealthier, and more peaceful place. He urges us to look beyond headlines and recognize that the state of the world is constantly improving. There has never been a better time to be alive, and while the path ahead may double back a few miles before finding its way again, I do believe that the future will be even better. I also believe that Africa has a big role to play in that better future.

Reading this book you might get the impression that I don't think that Africa is currently on track. That would be wrong. I do, and it is, but I also believe it could be traveling down that path much faster than it is currently moving. With more digitalization, and with the better governance and greater opportunities that technology can bring, the people of sub-Saharan Africa could follow the path set by China and develop rapidly—instead of at its current pace—into a connected region of middle-income countries.

I hope that this book will help to add more focus on tech investments in Africa and persuade investors, both private and public, to allocate capital to those areas where it can improve the region's digital environment and have the greatest impact. I also want to share my experience and help other investors looking at Africa, as well as local entrepreneurs building their businesses, to know what to expect, to understand where the risks lie, and to increase their odds of success. As Africa increases its rate of success, we all benefit.

In writing this book, I interviewed a number of experts, entrepreneurs, and business leaders in the region and I am grateful for all their help. Special thanks go to Phil Parker, Jasjit Singh, Kresten Buch, Ranjith Cherickel, Ann Rosenberg, Ole Hansen, Herman Singh, Sabrina Dorman, Martin Nielsen, Martin Majlund, Christian Grubak, Daniel Maison and Toby Clements as a great inspirer. Dean Shanson helped me to put my ideas and experiences into words, and a very special thanks goes to my lovely family, who have both endured my frequent travels and shared my love of Africa. Any errors are, of course, my own.

Finally, it is important to point out that this book is not meant to be an academic publication. It draws on my own experience, on interviews, and on secondary data to present a picture of the current investment environment in sub-Saharan Africa, its opportunities, its challenges, and its risks. No book, including this one, can ever hope to show all of the complexity of Africa. I hope that this book, however, can help investors and entrepreneurs understand what it takes to succeed in the region, and what sub-Saharan Africa needs to develop even faster.

Introduction

Is Sub-Saharan Africa the Next China?

Over the last twenty years, the world has witnessed the impact of one of history's most remarkable stories of economic growth. A country once characterized by rice paddies, heavy industry, and state control of the economy has become a dynamic, modern economy. Cities that once rang to the sound of bicycle bells now hum with electric mopeds powered by the latest rechargeable battery technology. Gleaming malls in Shanghai sell goods by Adidas and Apple, Burberry and Bulgari. Car parks in Shenzhen contain Porsches and Maseratis parked alongside the Volkswagens, Hondas, and Toyotas favored by the middle classes.

China still has some poverty, of course, and plenty of inequality, but it is possible to talk of a middle class with a disposable income that enables it to buy international brands, take international flights, visit Disneyland, dine in restaurants, and pay for leisure activities. The economy is no longer dependent on agriculture and steel production. Its technology firms produce world-class mobile phones, world-beating 5G technology, and social media software that has revolutionized communications—and captured the attention of teenagers from Fujian to Florida.

China has changed. It might still be led by a "communist" government with increasingly authoritarian tendencies but in releasing the power of private enterprise, it has transformed itself into the world's second-largest economy. Hundreds of millions of people have seen their lives improved. Children born in Xian, Chongqing, and Chengdu have opportunities now that their parents and grandparents could only have dreamed of.

For investors who put funds into companies like Tencent, Huawei, and Alibaba, the financial rewards have been tremendous. The $20 million that Softbank invested in Alibaba in 2000 was worth almost $125 billion at the start of 2020.[1] A private investor who bought HKD$10,000 of Tencent shares in 2004 would have had over HKD$5 million at the end of 2020. When growth comes that fast, it generates plenty of rewards for everyone.

More importantly, though, it also gives those investors a sense that their capital has done more than generate returns. It's helped to transform a region and build companies that have improved the lives of millions.

Changes like the one that China has undergone over the last couple of decades are rare, but they show what can happen—and the pace at which that change can happen—when the circumstances are right.

Those circumstances may now be right in sub-Saharan Africa.

The Challenge—and Opportunity—of Africa

To talk of sub-Saharan Africa is to describe a vast, complex region. Even if you exclude the eight largely Arabic-speaking north African countries that mostly line the Mediterranean coast, we are still talking about over a billion people in 46 countries, scattered across more than 23.6 million square kilometers—a size large enough to fit all of the United States, Canada, and the EU combined.

The continent has more than 2,000 recognized languages; more than a third of the world's languages are in sub-Saharan Africa alone. The continent may have transnational *lingua franca*—Arabic, English, French, Swahili in East Africa—but individual countries can have multiple languages within their borders: South Africa alone has eleven, including Ndebele, Sepede, Xhosa, and Zulu.

It's also disparate. China is a single political entity with the same time zone from the Indian border to the edge of Korea. Europe might

---

[1] Kristina Zucchi, "The Top 5 Alibaba Shareholders," Investopedia, updated January 13, 2020 https://www.investopedia.com/articles/investing/111114/top-five-alibaba-shareholders.asp#:~:text=Softbank%20Group&text=Softbank%20invested%20%2420%20million%20in,now%20worth%20nearly%20%24125%20billion

have multiple countries but moving goods from one end of the continent to the other is now simple and fast, especially within the area of the European Union, an organization dedicated to the free flow of people and goods within its borders. Africa, in theory, should have the world's biggest free trade area. In March 2018, leaders of 44 African countries signed the African Continental Free Trade Agreement (AfCFTA) in Kigali, Rwanda. Signatories are supposed to remove tariffs on at least 90 percent of their goods over the next five to ten years.

It's an ambitious and positive goal. Despite an alphabet soup of different regional trade groups—the Common Market for Eastern and Southern Africa (COMESA), the East African Community (EAC), the Economic Community of West African States (ECOWAS), the Community of Sahel-Saharan States (CSSS) to name just a few—African countries currently trade very little among themselves. While intra-regional trade makes up 59 percent of exports in Asia and 69 percent in Europe, only around 17 percent of the exports of African countries go to other African countries. It's easier for an African country to sell their commodities—and it's usually commodities, rather than products or services—to Europe or to Asia than to sell them to their own neighbors.[2]

Nor is it just tariffs that currently prevent products flowing smoothly across the African continent. Different standards in each country means that a company in one country can expect to create different versions of the same product to sell to different countries in the same area. *The Economist* has described how a large South African retailer with stores across the continent has a warehouse where it removes toothpaste from cartons used in one country to pack the tubes into new cartons for sale in countries with different labelling rules.[3]

An African entrepreneur may look at his continent and see a giant land mass filled with potential customers with a need for his product. He might dream of his product being sold in every city from Cape Town to

---

[2] "Economic Development in Africa Report 2019: Made in Africa: Rules of origin for enhanced intra-African trade," UNCTAD, June 26, 2019 https://unctad.org/en/pages/PressRelease.aspx?OriginalVersionID=520

[3] "Forty-four African countries sign a free-trade deal," The Economist, March 22, 2018 https://www.economist.com/middle-east-and-africa/2018/03/22/forty-four-african-countries-sign-a-free-trade-deal

Casablanca, but he'll also be aware that entering each of those markets means understanding each country's tariffs, regulations, and additional informal trade restrictions like customs issues. And that's before he's figured out how to move his goods from the factory to the wholesaler along potholed roads that might be washed out in the rainy season and through checkpoints that demand unofficial tolls and high taxes. It isn't even easy for him to travel to those countries to find out for himself what he needs to do to penetrate those markets. Only a quarter of African countries allow visa-free entry to citizens of other African countries.[4] Add those countries that provide visas on arrival and still around half the continent requires the entrepreneur to apply for a visa before he can travel to meet potential partners and scout locations.

Each of those obstacles—tariffs, standards, and restrictions on free travel—combine with poor infrastructure, multiple languages and, of course, the vast distances to make talk of "Africa" as a single economic bloc, let alone a "market," unrealistic. Africa is a continent, not a country, and a collection of trading blocs with multiple overlapping agreements rather than a place with anything approaching a single policy towards trade or finance or doing business.

But it does at least have a vision of a different future.

In January 2015, the African Union adopted Agenda 2063. The agenda was first described in 2013, so it's a 50-year goal to improve economic development and end poverty within a generation. Flagship projects include the establishment of an integrated high speed train network to connect all African capitals and commercial centers. An African commodities strategy aims to turn Africa from an exporter of raw materials into a continent that processes its own ores. A single African Air-Transport Market is supposed to improve economic integration and liberalize air transport services. It envisages an African Investment Bank with headquarters in Tripoli, Libya and Yaoundé, Cameroon, as well as a Pan-African Stock Exchange, an African Monetary Fund, and an African Central Bank. It even has a cyberspace strategy.

---

[4] Visa Openness Index, Africa Visa Openness Report 2019, African Development Bank Group, African Union, November 2019
https://www.visaopenness.org/fileadmin/uploads/afdb/Documents/visa-openness-2019.pdf

Introduction

It's easy to be cynical about a fifty-year plan that includes an African strategy for outer space, let alone cyberspace, and about an imminent plan to put a transcontinental investment bank in war-torn Tripoli, but initiatives like Agenda 2063 do show that Africa is not in stasis. The AfCFTA is part of Agenda 2063, and within four months, had added five more signatories to the 44 who signed in Kigali. By the end of 2019, 54 countries had signed; only Eritrea has held out. In 2016, only nine countries provided eVisa platforms. Currently 21 countries do. All the countries of ECOWAS now have reciprocal visa policies, as do 60 percent of the EAC and the UMA.

Some countries are doing better than others. In 2019, Harvard's Center for International Development took the latest global trade data and used it to predict growth rates over the next ten years. It found that Libya, a country now blighted by civil war, was predicted to grow by less than half a percent even before the effects of Covid-19, less than Venezuela. The Democratic Republic of Congo would beat the prediction if it managed more than just 2.05 percent, and Algeria, despite being right next to Tunisia, was expected to achieve less than half its neighbor's growth rate. And yet Harvard also expected that seven of the fifteen fastest-growing economies in the world in the next decade would be in Africa.[5] Uganda and Egypt would top the list but Tanzania, Mali, Mozambique, and Tunisia could all expect growth rates of at least 5 percent. Movement may be uneven but it's present—and the road has already been traveled.

Africa Is Young and Increasingly Digital

Thirty years ago, China's economic situation was similar to sub-Saharan Africa's. Measured in current US dollars, gross domestic product in both China and across sub-Saharan Africa was around $350 billion in 1990.

Between then and 2019, China's GDP grew to reach more than $14 trillion. Sub-Saharan Africa's barely reached $1.8 trillion; China had grown

---

[5] Chuck McKenney, "India Slowing, China Resilient in Harvard's New Global Growth Projections," Atlas of Economic Complexity, June 3, 2019 https://atlas.cid.harvard.edu/growth-projections

eight times faster. Measured by GDP per capita the results are even stronger: the population of sub-Saharan Africa more than doubled over that period while the population of China "only" increased by 22 percent.[6]

Sub-Saharan Africa has clearly missed an opportunity, but does it have another opportunity to enjoy rapid growth now? If China can grow and transform that quickly, is sub-Saharan Africa—despite its borders and tariffs—ready now to do the same?

There are at least a couple of reasons to believe that sub-Saharan Africa might just be on the verge of the same kind of breakout that China has enjoyed over the last two or three decades.

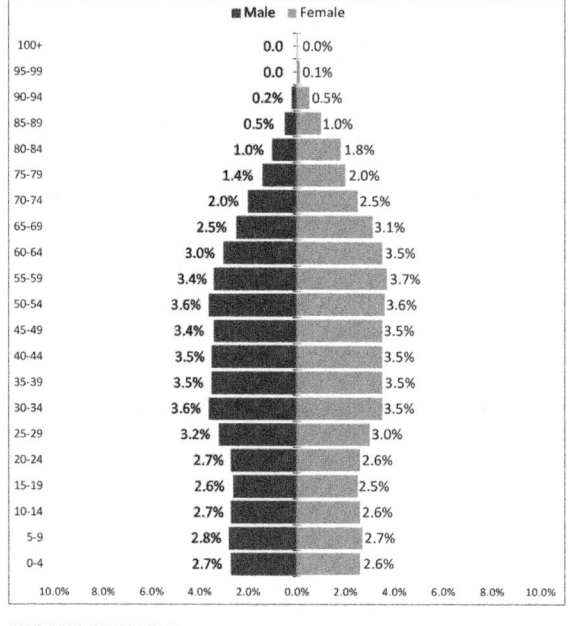

EUROPE - 2019
Population: 747,182,815

---

[6] "GDP (current US$) - Sub-Saharan Africa, China," The World Bank, accessed September 15, 2020 https://data.worldbank.org/indicator/NY.GDP.MKTP.CD?end=2019&locations=ZG-CN&start=1990

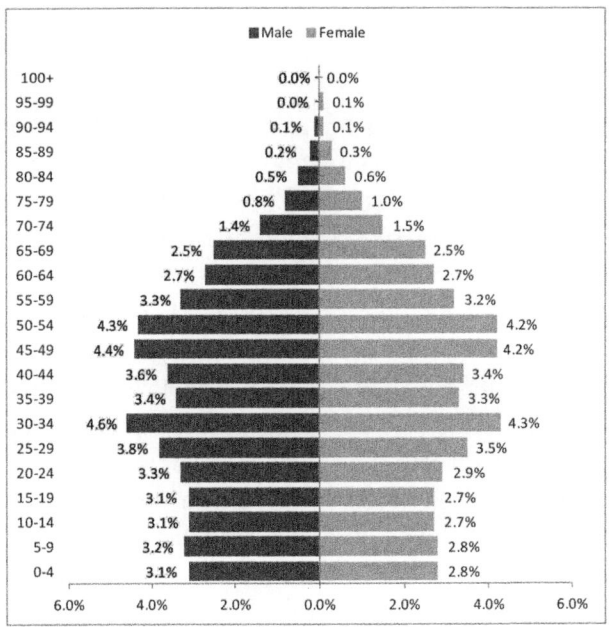

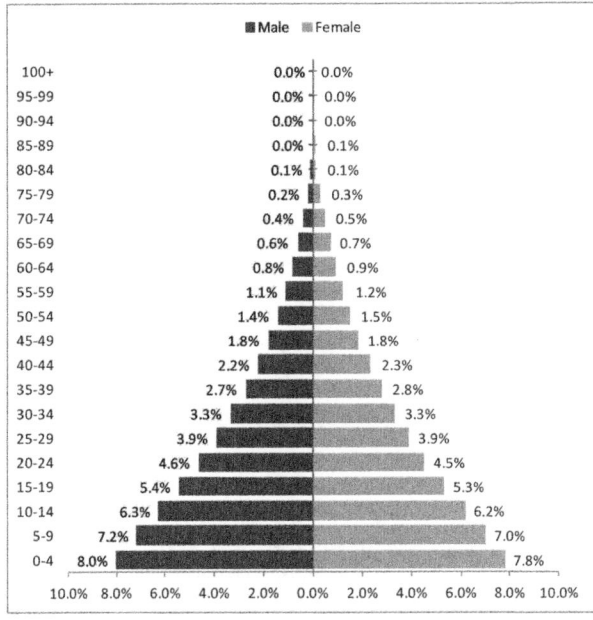

Figure 1. Population pyramids of Europe, China and Sub-Saharan Africa (www.populationpyramid.net)

The first is demographic.

Europe's population is ageing. According to the latest data from the European Commission, the population of the EU will peak at 525 million people in 2044 then fall to 408 million by the end of the century. At the same time, the percentage of working age people in the EU will fall from 65 percent in 2018 to just 55 percent in 2100.[7] By the end of the century almost half of Europe's population will depend on the income generated by the other half.

In China, the situation is no better. The population is already shrinking. The country's official fertility rate is 1.6 children per woman, a long way below the replacement rate of 2.1 children per woman. Unofficially, the figure may be as low as 1.18.[8] In 2016, the country tried to increase population growth by ending its one-child policy and raising the limit to two children per family. It didn't help. In 2018, the total number of births in China fell 12 percent compared to the previous year. They declined again the following year. From a country of four grandparents and two parents doting on a single child, China is rapidly moving to couples with four elderly parents to care for as well as their own child. That will have consequences for both productivity and consumer spending. China may be booming now but it faces a demographic challenge: a shrinking working-age population and a large ageing cohort.

Africa, however, is still growing. The population of sub-Saharan Africa increases by 2.7 percent a year. Every twelve months Africa adds the equivalent of a country the size of Canada to its demographic total. By 2050, the continent's population is expected to double. It's on track to reach 2.5 billion people, a quarter of the world's population, by the middle of the century.[9] While the market in Europe is currently richer

---

[7] "The EU's population projected up to 2100," *Eurostat*, July 10, 2019 https://ec.europa.eu/eurostat/web/products-eurostat-news/-/DDN-20190710-1

[8] Steven Lee Myers, Jin Wu, and Claire Fu, "China's Looming Crisis: A Shrinking Population," New York Times, updated January 17, 2020, https://www.nytimes.com/interactive/2019/01/17/world/asia/china-population-crisis.html

[9] "Africa's population will double by 2050," *The Economist,* March 26, 2020 https://www.economist.com/special-report/2020/03/26/africas-population-will-double-by-2050

Introduction

than Africa's and the population of Asia is four times bigger, both look likely to decline, age, and spend less on consumer goods. As Hans Rosling describes in his book *Factfulness*,[10] Africa's birth rate may fall as women's education levels rise and the continent becomes wealthier but compared to the rest of the world, it's still a young and growing market.

It's also an increasingly sophisticated market. The second important factor that has led some analysts to put sub-Saharan Africa on the edge of rapid growth is the increasing use of mobile technology.

According to the latest report by GSMA, an association of global mobile operators, sub-Saharan Africa had 456 million unique mobile subscribers at the start of 2019, a subscriber penetration rate of 44 percent. It is also adding to that number faster than any other region. By 2025, the association estimates, the subscriber base in sub-Saharan Africa will top 600 million, about half the population.[11]

That rate varies by country and also by age group. In Kenya, 70 percent of the population under the age of 30 has some sort of mobile subscription. In Nigeria, 152 million of its estimated 187 million people have a mobile subscription, including 72 percent of the population under the age of 30. In Uganda, that young market penetration rate is as high as 75 percent.

"Across the region, the demographic bulge will result in large numbers of young consumers becoming adults and owning a mobile phone for the first time," GSMA's report says. "This segment of the population will account for the majority of new mobile subscribers and, as 'digital natives,' will significantly influence mobile usage patterns in the future."

It's that combination of an almost uniquely young and growing population coupled with the opportunities that technology offers for digital banking, online marketing, real-time information, and Internet consumption that makes Africa so attractive now.

---

[10] Hans Rosling, with Ola Rosling and Anna Rosling Rönnlund, *Factfulness: Ten Reasons We're Wrong About The World - And Why Things Are Better Than You Think,* Sceptre, 2018

[11] GSMA, *The Mobile Economy: Sub-Saharan Africa,* 2019 https://www.gsma.com/mobileeconomy/sub-saharan-africa/

A region filled with young people ready to build start-ups and consume digital services is a region on the edge of a valuable opportunity. Some of that opportunity is already being exploited and is yielding rewards. As we'll see in this book, M-Pesa, a digital banking service launched in Kenya and Tanzania by Vodafone and Safaricom in 2007, has allowed parts of Africa that have never had bank accounts to engage with the financial system. It's made financial transactions easier, enabled small business owners to pay suppliers and receive payments, and increased social security. The service has since inspired competitors, grown across the region, and spread to South Africa, India, and Afghanistan among other countries. The ability to make online tax payments has improved transparency and enabled some states to shrink the black economy. The spread of handheld devices on which people can communicate, consume content, and place orders enables entrepreneurs to create businesses that sell services from entertainment to education, reach vast markets, and enjoy the same economies of scale that have allowed digital companies such as Amazon and Alibaba to become multi-billion dollar businesses. According to one study, transactions via mobile wallets and phones now represent 87 percent of Kenya's GDP, and 82 percent of Ghana's. That puts Kenya only behind China, which transfers as much as 125 percent of its GDP through mobile payments each year, including person-to-person transfers.[12] But the same study shows massive differences across Africa as on average transactions via mobile wallets and phones now only represent 21 percent of African GDP — or only 16.8% of the level in China.

For any investor who wants their capital to do more than deliver returns, who wants it to have an impact that changes people's lives, sub-Saharan Africa might appear challenging and difficult but it also appears to offer the same promise of both financial and impact returns that China once offered and which few other places in the world can rival. Sub-Saharan Africa is ready for investors who can help fund the

---

[12] Tijsbert Creemers, Thiruneeran Murugavel, Frédéric Boutet, Othman Omary, and Takeshi Oikawa, "Five Strategies for Mobile-Payment Banking in Africa," BCG.com, August 13, 2020 https://www.bcg.com/en-il/publications/2020/five-strategies-for-mobile-payment-banking-in-africa

digital businesses that can power the entire region through the twenty-first century.

This book is about what I've learned building companies and leading investment rounds in sub-Saharan Africa over five years. As I've divided my time between Denmark, Kenya, and South Africa (as well as many of the other nations that make up the region's 46 countries) I've learned what it's really like to try to build technology businesses in the region, where the obstacles lie, and the adjustments that investors and entrepreneurs have to make for the region.

I've found that sub-Saharan Africa's development stage—its ability to make use of the technology that's available to it—is overrated compared to many people's expectations. From funding and planning to recruitment and scaling, the risks and the challenges faced by entrepreneurs in sub-Saharan Africa are unique and need to be understood by any investor thinking of putting funds into the region. But the opportunity is also highly underestimated. Investments carefully chosen and skillfully managed, and that emphasize digitalization, can indeed produce impressive results both for investors and for the region and these opportunities will only grow in the future.

I'll start by looking broadly at the opportunity available in Africa.

One common mistake among investors in the region is to assume that the middle class entrepreneurs they meet in Kenyan cities and in Johannesburg cafes are representative of the region as a whole. They miss the deprivation of Africa's subsistence farmers, who still make up 65 percent of the continent's population.[13] They misjudge sub-Saharan Africa's heterogeneity, and as they underestimate the area's future potential, they also overestimate its current development. Africa may be growing an increasingly digital middle class but 645 million people in the region still lack access to electricity.[14] According to the United Nations, of the 763 million people living on less than $1.90 a day in 2015, the

---

[13] Isadora Savage, "10 Facts About Farming in Africa," The Borgen Project, June 27, 2019 https://borgenproject.org/tag/subsistence-farming/

[14] *African Economic Outlook 2017: Entrepreneurship and Industrialisation,* African Development Bank Group, OECD Development Centre, and UNDP, 2017 https://www.afdb.org/fileadmin/uploads/afdb/Documents/Publications/AEO_2017_Report_Full_English.pdf

latest figures available, 413 million of them were in sub-Saharan Africa. A third of the region's employed workers lived on less than that amount in 2018, and forecasts suggests that without "significant shifts in policy," the portion of the region's population living in extreme poverty by 2030 will still be in double figures.[15]

My experience matching investors with entrepreneurs has taken place largely in the region's most developed hubs in Kenya and South Africa, and together with co-investors in Nigeria. I'll describe the opportunity that I've found available in sub-Saharan Africa, but I also won't flinch from explaining the challenges of its current stage of development.

Having discussed the area, I'll then talk about impact investing.

Investing that looks beyond financial returns has a long history. It also has a broad definition that can range from ETF-screened ESG/SRI funds that claim to be socially responsible but are actually little different to traditional investments, to the work of NGOs that are closer to charitable contributions.

I don't intend to tell people how or why they should spend their money. Everyone will have their own investment priorities. But I do want to ensure that people make their investments with their eyes open, especially when their priority is that their investments do more than deliver a financial return, as many investors in Africa do.

Currently, too much impact investment is purpose-driven and not impact-driven. It's designed to make investors feel good rather than make a difference that can be felt by the people that investment is supposed to affect. I will explore the definition of "impact" and the importance of distinguishing between a drive for satisfaction about oneself and one's work, and the achievements that those efforts bring.

A key argument in the book is that the biggest impact an investor can make in sub-Saharan Africa is through digitalization. It's technology that can drive down marginal costs, increase transparency, improve government, and build trust. It's digitalization that can help farmers bring their goods to market and receive a fair price, help urban sellers

---

[15] *The Sustainable Development Goals Report 2019,* United Nations Statistics Division https://unstats.un.org/sdgs/report/2019

find new buyers and track their sales, and make it harder for officials to take bribes without being seen.

A technology company has the potential to cross borders, deliver a transregional service, and grow from a small company to a giant firm with a large valuation that can change life in Africa to the same extent that WeChat and Alibaba have changed life in China.

But changing Africa through technology is not as simple as designing and releasing a mobile application. Sub-Saharan Africa is not Silicon Valley. Tech companies in the region struggle to raise funds in seed and Series A rounds. Capital is a scarce resource, bureaucracy is stifling, taxes disincentivize effort and investment, and work permits are difficult to obtain for foreign talent. Other regions, such as Singapore, Israel, and Estonia, have been much better at clearing the obstacles. Impact investment funds in the region still tend to flow towards asset-heavy areas such as healthcare, energy, and banking when they should also be flowing towards tech companies, to e-learning, govtech, health-tech, ecommerce, fintech, content, etc. I will look at the special challenges of identifying and making impact investments in sub-Saharan Africa, with an emphasis on digitalization.

How to Build a Sub-Saharan Start-Up

The second section of the book is made up largely of what it takes to build a successful start-up in the challenging environment of sub-Saharan Africa. I start by discussing the tech investment eco-system in the region and describe the challenges that businesses and investors face as they try to create start-ups.

While countries like Singapore and Israel have worked hard to create an environment in which tech entrepreneurs can thrive, few of the countries of sub-Saharan have implemented policies that attempt to fill skills gaps or attract capital. There are few, if any, government programs to match skilled but inexperienced employees to new companies, and little support for founders with ideas and enthusiasm but few resources.

I'll explain the challenge of finding digital talent in sub-Saharan Africa, and in particular of funding the businesses that that talent wants to build.

I'll then get into detail. The process of creating a business anywhere begins with an idea, so I'll explain how a business idea should be born, selected and refined, and using case studies derived from my own businesses in the region—including a digital music service and a beauty firm—I'll discuss how those ideas need to adapt to sub-Saharan Africa.

One particularly popular way to implement a business idea in Africa is take an idea that's already worked elsewhere. Mdundo, the digital music service I helped to develop, is a kind of Spotify for Africa but it's had to make a number of adjustments to match Africa's markets and limitations. I'll explain idea replication, what it needs, and what investors and entrepreneurs hoping to copy an idea in Africa need to consider.

I'll also discuss business models in that chapter: what they contain and how they need to adjust when faced with African conditions.

Two of the biggest challenges that I've come across in sub-Saharan Africa, in addition to funding, are recruitment and partnerships. Africa has high unemployment but it also has a skills gap, a weak education system, and a lack of certification. That makes it difficult for employers to find the staff they need, while the debts and obligations those staff face outside the workplace often make working for a start-up less attractive than a more reliable job in a large company or a government position. Motivation and trust are particularly important issues when building businesses in sub-Saharan Africa. I'll explain what investors and entrepreneurs need to consider.

And while partnerships are often an important element in smoothing the growth of a new business, in sub-Saharan Africa, those partnerships have to be forged without the safety net of a reliable legal system. If they don't work for both parties, they won't work at all.

The Present and the Future of Sub-Saharan Africa

The last two chapters of the book take a broader look at the region: its current state and its future direction.

Africa is changing but it's not changing evenly or as quickly as it could. Technology and digitalization are transforming some places and leaving others almost untouched. Those changes will continue— and the opportunities they create will continue to grow. A region with a ballooning, young population, increasing familiarity with mobile and digital technology, and a drive to succeed does have the potential to change the continent in the same way that China has changed over the last generation and a half.

In the time that I've spent in Africa, I've seen that potential. I've seen the energy, drive, and commitment of the entrepreneurs of Kinshasa, Cape Town, and Nairobi. I've watched them battle bureaucracy and poor infrastructure, and I've seen them find innovative ways to reach and serve their customers and clients. Many are succeeding. Despite all of the challenges, despite the difficulties of sourcing funds, building teams, and communicating a brand across different markets and different languages, they are making use of digitalization to lower their costs and build not just new businesses but new business models suited to their contexts.

But too many are also failing, and far too many are missing the opportunity to try. Sub-Saharan Africa has potential but currently that potential is unfulfilled. Local capital created through real estate, mining, and construction returns to those industries instead of moving to more transformative technology firms. Foreign private capital lacks the knowledge to assess country risk across sub-Saharan Africa, and development funds are incapable of assessing the project risk of local technology companies. If sub-Saharan Africa is going to make the most of this moment and reap the benefits that a young, digital-savvy population can produce, those funds need to change their strategies and put their money where private investors currently fear to invest.

In *Capitalism and Freedom,* Milton Friedman described the purpose of a corporation. "There is one and only one social responsibility of business," he wrote, "to use its resources and engage in activities designed to increase its profits so long as it stays within the rules of the game, which is to say, engages in open and free competition without deception or fraud."[16]

Today's investors and entrepreneurs want more. We want the capital we provide and the rewards we create to also do good. We want the businesses we build to improve lives and lift regions. At the very least,

---

[16] Milton Friedman, *Capitalism and Freedom: Fortieth Anniversary Edition,* (University of Chicago Press, 2002), 133

we want to know that we've built companies that deliver services that people want, create employment, and pay taxes.

In August 2019, America's Business Roundtable, an association of the chief executives of the country's leading corporations, released a statement describing a new "purpose of a corporation."[17] Corporations, argued the 181 signatories of the roundtable, have a commitment "to all of our stakeholders." The signatories committed to deliver value to customers; invest in employees; deal fairly and ethically with suppliers; support the communities in which they work; and generate long-term value for shareholders.

Few places in the world offer a greater opportunity to deliver a positive impact to large numbers of stakeholders than sub-Saharan Africa.

It's a region that has both challenges and potential. Investments carefully chosen and skillfully managed, and that emphasize digitalization and technology that can lower marginal costs, can produce results, both for investors and for the area. There is an opportunity in Africa for investors to make healthy returns and to place funds in an area where they can make a real difference in the same way that early investors in China's development have reaped rewards for both themselves and for hundreds of millions of people.

Currently, that opportunity is not being exploited. This book explains why it's being missed and what needs to happen to make the most of it.

---

[17] Business Roundtable, *Statement on the Purpose of a Corporation,* August 19, 2019 https://opportunity.businessroundtable.org/wp-content/uploads/2020/03/BRT-Statement-on-the-Purpose-of-a-Corporation-with-Signatures.pdf

Chapter One

The African Entrepreneurial Opportunity

My first business trip to Africa was in 2014 but that wasn't the first time I had visited the continent. In 1999, I had spent a couple of months backpacking through South Africa, and traveling across Namibia, Botswana, and Zimbabwe. That was when I had first seen what Africa had to offer: its endless natural landscapes, its incredible wildlife, its enormous potential. In 2002, I returned, heading this time to East Africa. Over six weeks, I got to know the best of Kenya and Tanzania. I went on safari. I climbed Kilimanjaro. I scuba dived and caught deep sea fish in the Indian Ocean. I saw the region and talked to people I met there, and in each place I visited I found a continent that was vibrant and dynamic, and beautiful too.

There are few things in life more exciting than experiencing new cultures, seeing new sights, and meeting people whose life and outlook are so different to your own.

But there's a difference between traveling through a region and doing business in one. In Denmark, life is orderly. We line up for tickets, and when we say that an event will start at eight, it will start at exactly eight. One lesson that every traveler learns quickly is that lines do not run straight in every part of the world, and scheduled times, whether they're train departures or appointments with officials, are often closer to approximations than fixed hours.

Those cultural clashes become stories that travelers share. For investors, though, they become cautionary tales that can raise the risk of their investments. They can create false expectations and build disappointment. It's always easier and safer to work in an area that you know and understand, a place that's familiar.

That was the path that lay open to me before I made that first business trip to Africa. I had spent ten years as a management consultant, working with businesses in the Nordic region. Those years had been enjoyable and successful. I had achieved what I had set out to do. KPMG had acquired my last business—a management consulting firm that had grown to employ a hundred people—and they wanted me to stay on as an equity partner.

It was tempting. There's no question it would have given me a very comfortable life. The next thirty or forty years would have been very clear. But...I didn't want to do it. I just couldn't see myself in that role. There were bigger things that I still wanted to do.

I just didn't know what those things were.

I invested in a software company and in mental health services. We built them up and sold them on but I wanted something with more impact and potential. Europe was flat and I was looking for something with bigger growth rates. I started to think about emerging markets.

South and Central America were options. I'd enjoyed trips to Venezuela, Mexico, and Guatemala but I don't speak Spanish or Portuguese. Flights from Europe are long and difficult, and the time difference makes a cross-oceanic business particularly hard to run from Europe. There were opportunities in Asia, of course, but what did I have to bring to the table? Plenty of smart people were already operating in that area. The more I thought about Africa, though, the more I felt its attraction. There are no big time zone differences to worry about. English is widely spoken. I would always be happy to return there. It's a continent that has always impressed me. There's no shortage of untapped resources in Africa, especially human resources. The growth rate looked tremendous, and I believed in Africa's potential. I was aware that there were risks, massive risks, but I was also aware that there are risks in doing nothing too.

I started investigating, and in hindsight I probably did what a lot of people do before they invest in the continent. I looked at the growth rates instead of at the absolute numbers and when you do that, it's easy to believe that Africa is already on exactly the same path that Asia has taken. You start to assume that at least some parts of Africa beyond South Africa are about to resemble Shanghai or Shenzhen or Seoul—

maybe not today, but the direction is clear. You see only the opportunity. You miss the details, and you miss the limited buying power. As I was to discover, Africa is more complicated than the headline figures suggest.

I started screening companies from a distance. I read business plans and met with founders in Europe who were creating businesses in Africa. There were plenty of interesting ideas: fintech projects, ecommerce stores, even small mom-and-pop stores looking for loans. But either the idea wasn't quite there or the founders weren't. Nothing caught my eye.

The change came during a lunch with Lasse Bolander, the chairman of Coop, Denmark's biggest retailer. Lasse was on the board of my last consulting business, and he had always been bullish on Africa. Whenever we got together, we would always talk about the continent and its opportunities.

"You should talk to Kresten Buch," he told me after I had described the difficulties I was having finding suitable African investments. "He's doing some very interesting things in Kenya."

Kresten Buch was a Dane who had taken a course in entrepreneurship at Stanford in 2009. He had met someone there from a Kenyan telecommunications company and had heard about East Africa's impressive mobile penetration. He decided that he just had to do something in the region. He had raised a small seed fund, headed to Kenya, and built an accelerator program, naming the program 88mph after a line in the Spielberg movie *Back to the Future*. Showing off his DeLorean time machine, Dr. Emmett Brown turns to Marty McFly and says: "If my calculations are correct, when this baby hits 88 miles per hour, you're gonna see some serious shit."

Kenya, Kresten believed, was ramping up towards 88 miles per hour and when it got there, it was going to show the world some serious shit. Kresten wanted to be there when it happened. I liked the sound of that.

I contacted Kresten, booked a flight on Turkish Airlines, and headed to Nairobi to meet his team and discover how I could help Africa's entrepreneurs.

88mph work-space in Nairobi

Entrepreneurship in Africa

When we talk of entrepreneurs in Europe or the United States, we tend to imagine young people with backgrounds in technology. They might start businesses in their garages or at a shared WeWork table, work all night, and dream of selling their new social media application or their data mining software to Google for giant sums of money. (In fact, they're just as likely to be late middle-aged baby boomers who have had enough of working for corporate America and want to spend their last productive years working for themselves while pursuing their passion.)[18]

As many as a third of working-age adults in sub-Saharan Africa are said to be either running a new business or trying to start one. Those figures compare to a sixth of Americans and only one in twenty

---

[18] "Boomers in Business—2020 Trends," Guidant Financial, last accessed September 15, 2020 https://www.guidantfinancial.com/small-business-trends/baby-boomer-business-trends/

Germans.[19] But most African entrepreneurs are not starting businesses because they're keen to work on their own terms or because they think they've spotted a gap in the market and hope that one day Jumia, an African ecommerce firm, or MTN, a telecom, will buy them out. They're doing it because they have little choice and no other opportunities.

The businesses they're running aren't built in air-conditioned offices or supported with venture capital funds protected by mentoring in a hi-tech accelerator. They're more likely to be a couple of plastic pallets, a sheet, and a range of different-colored sunhats. Or their assets will be a polystyrene box filled with flavored ice on the side of the road. Outside the cities, a successful business might look like a small shack made of timber and tarpaulin selling pots, pans, and packets of chewing gum. For Phil Parker, a professor of marketing at INSEAD, businesses like these are a miracle. They're able to reach the last mile and still make a profit. "No multinational can do that," he says. "They are extremely successful."

They may be successful. They may even be profitable, but they're to business creation what subsistence farming is to agriculture. They rarely employ anyone outside the family and they don't generate enough profits to allow for investment or growth. They're a way for an individual to avoid starvation in a country whose birth rate outstrips its growth rate.

More important to the future of sub-Saharan Africa are the businesses being developed by entrepreneurs whose visions are larger than a shack by the road. Those business-builders are trying to travel the same path taken by entrepreneurs everywhere but with little of the infrastructure to support them on the way. Some of them, despite the challenges, have been remarkably successful.

Mo Ibrahim represents one version of that entrepreneurship. Ibrahim was born in East Africa, and grew up in Egypt where his father worked for a cotton company. After graduating from Alexandria University with a degree in electrical engineering, he returned to Sudan and worked for the country's telephone company, Sudan Telecom. But it was only after he moved to England that Africa was able to make the most of Ibrahim's

---

[19] "Africa is full of schemes to help entrepreneurs," The Economist, October 3, 2019

expertise, his knowledge, and his entrepreneurialism. He completed a doctorate in mobile communications, then worked for BT, Britain's telecommunications company.

Even in developed economies, however, large companies have inefficiencies and bureaucracies, and after six years of fighting with committees and pushing for investment in mobile technologies, Ibrahim left and created a consultancy called MSI, or Mobile Systems International. He helped telecoms operators to increase their coverage using the minimum amount of hardware.

"Operators were spending billions, and if I could save them 10% on their network then I was saving hundreds of millions," he told *The Guardian* in 2009. "So we can charge what we like."[20]

He spun off a subsidiary called Celtel and sold the rest of the company to Marconi in 2000 for just under a billion dollars. Instead of designing systems that other operators would implement, Celtel would build the networks itself—and it would do it in a place that no one else wanted to enter. "I noticed—we noticed—that there was a big scramble for licenses everywhere, and countries had started to charge large sums of money to operators," he said. "The one place on earth where licenses were available for free was Africa. Nobody wanted to go in."

The result was the rapid spread of mobile technology in Africa, the creation of secondary businesses such as phone repair shops and charging stations, and greater transparency in issues from the price of sweet potatoes in different marketplaces to the counting of votes in elections. Celtel also acquired a reputation for cleanliness. Ibrahim stipulated that payments of over $30,000 needed the signature of the entire board, restricting the ability of governments and officials to demand secret bribes. Anyone demanding a million dollars to award a license would be told that the company's board would know about it. Officials stopped asking. In 2004, six years after the formation of the company and having transformed much of Africa, Ibrahim sold his second company for $3.4 billion, making many of his African employees millionaires.

---

[20] Geraldine Bedell, "The man giving Africa a brighter future," *The Guardian*, February 1, 2009 https://www.theguardian.com/lifeandstyle/2009/feb/01/mo-ibrahim

The African Entrepreneurial Opportunity

It's a story that says much about the potential of Africa. Mo Ibrahim is a product of the continent, and while he completed his education in England, his talent and his drive were formed in Africa. He was able to build a multi-billion dollar business because so much of the rest of the world failed to see the opportunity that Africa offered. There was no reason that Celtel shouldn't have faced tougher competition from older, foreign telecoms companies with more capital and deeper connections. But those companies had overlooked the potential of African growth. They were unwilling to take the risk and they missed the chance to cash in on a giant, developing market.

Other local entrepreneurs behave exactly like entrepreneurs everywhere. Etop Ikpe started his first business while he was an actuarial student at the University of Lagos. ClickMobile was an IT solution for companies that wanted to build apps to view their business data. In 2009, after graduating, he formed a fashion start-up called Three Stitches which he sold to DealDey, a Nigerian ecommerce business, three years later. He remained as the co-managing director at that company until it was bought by Konga, a rival ecommerce site, where he became the director of marketplace operations. He left that company just eight months later to help create Cars45, a start-up for which he raised $5 million in 2017.

Cars45 solves what Ikpe calls a "pan-African problem":[21] the difficulty of buying and selling used cars. Customers with a car to sell can use the company's website to arrange an appointment with one of the company's inspection centers. Cars45 then makes an offer and if the deal is accepted, wires the money to the seller's bank account within 45 minutes. Revenues come from fees earned when selling those cars to a network of private buyers but can also include inspection services, financing, and pricing services like Kelly's Bluebook.

Clearly, an easier way for Africa's car owners to sell their vehicles is not going to transform the continent in the way that a new mobile network can do. Etop Ikpe hasn't built a new way of transferring high speed

---

[21] ConnectNigeria.com, "MEET THE BOSS: ETOP IKPE CEO Cars45," YouTube video, January 9, 2020 https://www.youtube.com/watch?v=h5aAzIEOZJg

data or a new African search engine. His model relies on the network that Mo Ibrahim has already pioneered. But he has built a successful business, created jobs, and made the process of car ownership easier. Car owners know they can sell their old cars safely, fairly, and reliably. Buyers looking for used cars will have a brand they can trust. With the use of the technology that another entrepreneur has introduced, Ikpe's own entrepreneurialism has made life in Africa a little easier and built a successful business.

It's that combination of youthful drive and rising technology that's creating opportunities for local entrepreneurs like Etop Ikpe. But it's the environment in which those opportunities grow that makes exploiting those challenges so difficult. One important factor that can't be ignored, and that has made the difference between Africa's economy and the prospects of countries like China, is governance: the ability to set fair tax rates, collect those taxes, and use them in the best way possible.

Africa's Entrepreneurial Environment

In 2007, Mo Ibrahim used some of his money to establish a prize for achievement in African leadership. The prize can only be given to former African heads of state who were democratically elected, have served their constitutionally-mandated terms, demonstrated exceptional leadership, and have left office in the last three years. The aim was to recognize African leaders who "under challenging circumstances, have developed their countries and strengthened democracy and human rights for the shared benefit of their people, paving the way for sustainable and equitable prosperity."[22] The prize is intended to highlight role models for the continent while ensuring that Africa can continue to benefit from the experience of leaders who have already brought benefits to their own countries. The prize is $500,000 a year for ten years, $200,000 a year for life, and another $200,000 a year for ten years to be spent on useful projects.

---

[22] "Ibrahim Prize for Achievement in African Leadership," Mo Ibrahim Foundation, last accessed September 15, 2020 https://mo.ibrahim.foundation/prize

The African Entrepreneurial Opportunity

The first winner of the prize was President Joaquim Chissano of Mozambique, who received it for his achievements in rebuilding the country after the civil war. Nelson Mandela also received an honorary award that year. The following year the prize went to President Festus Mogae of Botswana. Other winners included President Pedro Pires of Cabo Verde and President Hifikipunye Pohamba of Namibia. The last winner was President Ellen Johnson Sirleaf of Liberia, the only female laureate, Africa's first female elected head of state, and a former Nobel prize-winner. That was in 2017. Over the prize's thirteen years, the judges have failed to find anyone worthy of the award on eight occasions. In March 2020, after announcing that there would be no winner for the second consecutive year, Mo Ibrahim tried to sound upbeat.

"Africa is facing some of the toughest challenges in the world—ranging from those connected to population growth, and economic development, to environmental impact," he said. "We need leaders who can govern democratically and translate these challenges into opportunities. With two-thirds of our citizens now living in better-governed countries than ten years ago, we are making progress. I am optimistic that we will have the opportunity to award this Prize to a worthy candidate soon."[23]

It's a statement that says much about the state of Africa. Governance is improving on the continent. Leaders like Festus Mogae and Ellen Johnson Sirleaf have shown that Africa can produce presidents who place their people and their countries ahead of their own personal finances. But it still happens too rarely. Freedom House ranks only five African countries as "free": South Africa, Namibia, Botswana, Ghana, and Tunisia. Twenty-three are rated "partly free," and the rest of the continent is not free at all.[24]

It's easy to blame history for Africa's governance problems, to put the continent's struggles down to the effects of colonialism and the

---

[23] "Mo Ibrahim Foundation announces no winner of 2019 Ibrahim Prize for Achievement in African Leadership," Mo Ibrahim Foundation, March 5, 2020 https://mo.ibrahim.foundation/sites/default/files/2020-03/2019-Ibrahim-Prize-press-release-EN.pdf

[24] "Countries and Territories," Freedom House, last accessed September 15, 2020 https://freedomhouse.org/countries/freedom-world/scores

imposition of borders that had little to do with boundaries respected by Africans themselves. But African countries have been independent for more than forty years now, and while the effects of that history can't be discounted, the decisions of Africa's own modern leaders have also played a large role. Different countries have applied different economic policies with predictable results. Zimbabwe's government nationalized productive land, gave it to cronies, then printed money to finance its debts. Between 1991 and 2008, its GDP declined from USD$8.6 billion to USD $4.4 billion.[25] Six years after the 1994 genocide, the Rwandan government implemented a Vision 2020 strategy that aimed to use the private sector to drive economic growth. The economy has since grown at a rate of about 7 percent a year.

Too few African leaders meet the criteria laid down by Mo Ibrahim's leadership prize. Too few are democratically elected. Too few leave office at the end of their terms. And too few demonstrate the exceptional leadership the continent demands—or even the kind of good governance that would allow entrepreneurs to take advantage of the opportunities that a growing, young population and a rise in technology can bring to Africa. In the meantime, that poor governance creates conditions that hold enterprises back.

When Cars45 started, the company would send people to inspect sellers' cars at their homes. Ikpe has described the difficulties—including the safety risks—of identifying serious sellers and verifying their vehicles. Databases were fragmented and official agencies wouldn't take seriously what the company was trying to do. Even finding dispatch riders to deliver clothes to Three Stitches' customers had been difficult.

Other businesses have run into problems of their own. Zumi, a Kenyan service that, after pivoting a few times, now connects clothing wholesalers and retailers, found that official duties and import taxes were cripplingly high. The company was left with three options: to pay the taxes in full and struggle to be competitive; to pay someone at the port to avoid paying the taxes altogether; or to pay someone a smaller

---

[25] "Zimbabwe," The World Bank, accessed September 15, 2020 https://data.worldbank.org/country/zimbabwe?view=chart

amount to reduce the taxes. In the end, the company chose to avoid working with imports altogether by focusing on selling goods already available in Kenya.

"To even be able to operate well as a business, you have to say: 'That is a world that I'm not going to touch and I will not be a player in that,'" explains co-founder Sabrina Dorman. "I will do business with those people. But my business can never touch that."

The African Century?

At his inauguration as president of South Africa in 1999, Thabo Mbeki talked of making "a contribution, however small, to the success of Africa's Renaissance." The next hundred years, he suggested would be "the African Century."

In the two decades since that speech, Africa *has* moved forward. The same entrepreneurial spirit that built places like Silicon Valley and that changed China flows through Africa. There's no shortage of young people on the continent who want to do more than sell hats from a plastic pallet or run a shack in a village. There is an understanding of what technology can do, how it can help a business to scale, and generate the transparency that any economy needs.

But at the same time there's also no shortage of problems. From distrust of sellers, including online retailers, to corruption, high taxes, ineffective government administration, and low purchasing power, entrepreneurs in sub-Saharan Africa face the kind of headwinds that aren't found anywhere else.

I was about to discover both the opportunities and the risks for myself. I arrived in Nairobi in the middle of the night and headed straight to 88mph's office. I heard about their portfolio of investments and listened to them explain how they were looking for companies in Africa that would make use of digitalization and grow. By the time I flew back out fifteen hours later, I knew that I was ready to invest in Africa.

Chapter Two

To Invest for Impact or for Growth?

I invested in Kresten's vehicle in Kenya. When Google encouraged Kresten to create an accelerator in South Africa, I invested in that too, as well as in the accelerator he launched in Nigeria. 88mph was spreading out, and in the process, it was introducing me to the variety—and the complexity—the region had to offer, as well as its needs. It's one thing to know that sub-Saharan Africa is a huge area; it's another to see for yourself how the differences between those regions affect investment opportunities and start-ups. There's nothing like investing your own money to bring that clarity

As I worked with Kresten, and in the portfolio of very early-stage startups that he and his team put together, I learned more, learned quickly, and I became more exposed to the continent. I was soon ready to start making direct investments of my own. I was beginning to do what I had hoped to do: to discover promising businesses in Africa and provide them with the funding and the help they needed to develop, grow, and scale.

The investment strategy that Mobile Africa (the working title for my investment portfolio) followed looked for investment targets with proven business models in a limited market, with a talented team. We supplied growth expertise, provided capital, and we opened access to a local network and international know-how. We also targeted investments in offline businesses if they included business model innovations related to Web or mobile access that produced scaling opportunities.

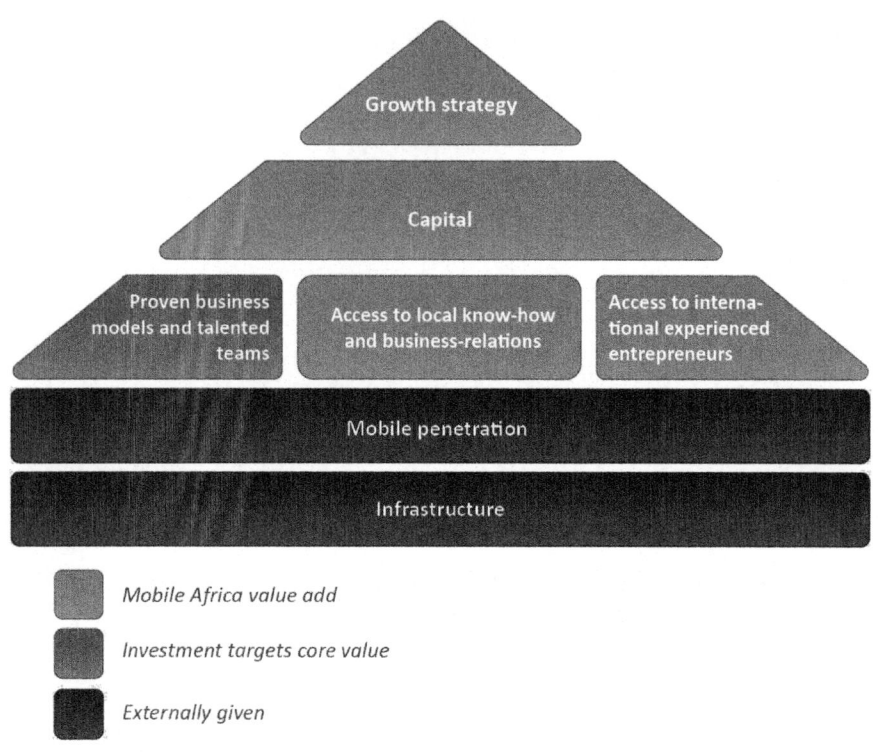

Figure 2. Value-creation house for Mobile Africa

Some of those investments were more successful than others. A placement in a bus ticketing service looked like it would produce healthy returns. Instead of walking down to the station and waiting to buy their tickets in person, travelers would be able to buy tickets for long distance buses online. The idea was sound; there's no shortage of similar services around the world. But the company died before the service started scaling.

Other investments did better. I'm now the chairman of Mdundo.com, a kind of Spotify for Africa. The platform's growth has shown just how far a good digital service can reach even in Africa's divided markets. Mdundo now influences more than 36 million listeners across the region, and more than twelve million annually in Kenya and Tanzania alone. Africa has a very rich musical tradition—music is one of the continent's biggest cultural assets—so being able to use digital technology to help artists find new audiences and earn richer rewards has been very satisfying. More than 80,000 artists have signed up, as well as some of the world's leading record labels, and their works are now available across the continent. Thanks to digitalization, a singer in Nigeria can now reach and profit from music fans in Kenya. Zambian kalindula music can reach paying audiences in Tanzania. It's a change to the industry that's already happened in Europe and the US, and it's a change that's now sweeping across African music, a very simple example of the impact that digitalization can have in Africa. We went public on Nasdaq in September 2020.

Mdundo.com ringing the bell at Nasdaq celebrating first day of trading. Due to Covid19, the local African Mdundo team could unfortunately not participate in the ceremony.

I also started an ecommerce business from scratch. BeautyClick attempts to replicate the work that Mayvenn has done in the United States, delivering wigs and hair extensions to African customers. That business has been challenging, and developing it has provided the strongest first-hand education that I could have found in the difficulties of entrepreneurship in sub-Saharan Africa. From sourcing products to building trust and loyalty and working with re-sellers, at each step of the development process I encountered challenges that were unique to the continent. I'll talk about those challenges in a future chapter, because it is essential to understanding what to expect when you grow a business in Africa from the ground up.

Investing for Impact

What I was trying to do in each of my investments in Africa was to build financially sustainable businesses. I wanted to help create companies that would provide employment, pay their taxes, deliver services to customers, and produce an above-average financial return. It's what investors everywhere want to do. It's what the businesses that I helped as a consultant in the Nordic countries wanted to do. But in places like Africa, investments often have a different goal.

When I started my consulting career almost twenty years ago, there was one buzzword that turned up all the time: synergies. Almost every pitch I heard and board meeting I attended would include at least one reference to the importance of building synergies. Get two or more organizations working together and you'll end up with something bigger than the sum of its parts. Businesses were looking for those opportunities—or at least, talking about them. In the last few years, "impact" and "impact investing" have taken over as the next great things and the most overused business buzzwords.

So what is impact investing and how does it differ from traditional investing?

Brian Trelstad, a Senior Lecturer at Harvard Business School, has placed impact investing on a "spectrum of capital."[26] The Omidyar Network, an investment group, has talked of an "Across the Returns

---

[26] Brian Trelstad, "Impact Investing: A Brief History," *Capitalism and Society:* Vol. 11: Iss. 2, Article 4. 2016

Continuum."[27] Jasjit Singh, Professor of Strategy at INSEAD, draws a "Force for Good Spectrum."[28] All are describing a line that places the traditional fiduciary investor with a focus on financial returns at one end, and philanthropy, with its focus on the public good, at the other end. Either an investor is looking to receive the highest possible financial returns their capital can generate for an accepted level of risk, or they're hoping to do the most "good" their money can buy.

The space between those extremes really started to fill in the late sixties and early seventies. "Socially responsible investing" broadened a path that had been laid decades earlier by religious groups who wanted to avoid businesses that produced social harm, such as alcoholism and gambling addiction. The new socially responsible investors, pressured by organizations such as unions, universities, and churches, looked to avoid investments in areas such as tobacco, arms, and apartheid South Africa. Today, says Trelstad, socially responsible investors use shareholder proxies to promote stronger corporate or environmental practices while screening out harmful investment areas such as strip-mining.

Impact investing lies somewhere in the middle of that spectrum. Like fiduciary investing, it expects to see a return on capital. But like philanthropy, it also puts social and environmental benefits at the forefront of the investment. An impact investor might look for projects that aim to reduce carbon dioxide emissions, that deliberately employ women in leadership positions, or whose goal is to create opportunities for micro entrepreneurs, for example.

---

[27] Matt Bannick, Paula Goldman, Michael Kubzansky, and Yasemin Saltuk, "Across the Returns Continuum," *Stanford Social Innovation Review*, Winter 2017, Volume 15, Number 1

[28] Jasjit Singh, "The Force for Good Spectrum: Using Business as a Tool," INSEAD Knowledge (blog), February 7, 2020 https://knowledge.insead.edu/blog/insead-blog/the-force-for-good-spectrum-using-business-as-a-tool-13321

Digital Africa

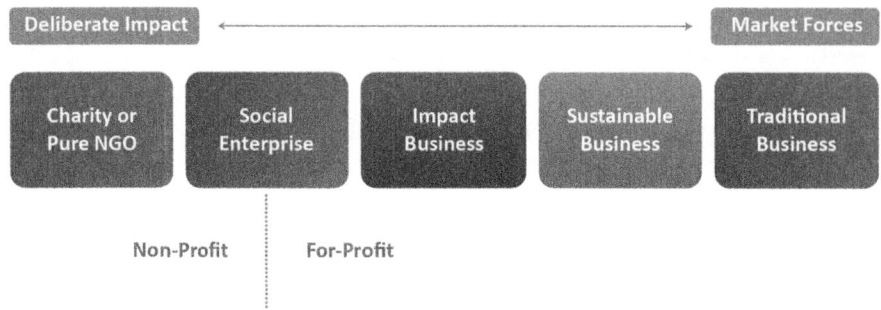

Figure 3. The force for Good Spectrum (Image, Jasjit Singh)

The success of the venture is measured by its financial returns but also by its non-financial benefits. That's the impact of the investment, and it allows investors to feel that they're making a particular kind of difference.

So investors start with a focus on placing their capital somewhere it can do some work. Their goals can then take two forms: a financial return, or a combination of financial return and impact. In turn, those investments that are also looking for an impact can deliver that impact in two ways. They can actively generate positive results, such as creating jobs or improving education; or, like ESG-screened funds, they can avoid negative effects by not investing in controversial weapons or neglecting health and safety.

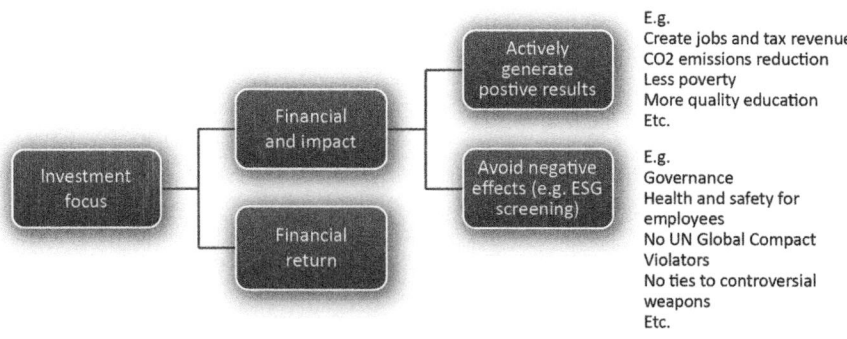

Figure 4. Illustrating the difference between actively generating positive results vs. avoiding negative effects

Jasjit Singh has defined **the effect of impact investing as the world with your involvement minus the world without your involvement**—a colorful way of describing the additionality that an impact investor brings. If the result of your involvement in the world is more jobs in a developing country or a small increase in an African country's tax revenue, then your investment has made a positive impact—but only if that investment wouldn't have happened without you. In a perfect capital market, with risk-adjusted returns at market-level, someone would have funded that project eventually: the world would have been the same without your involvement. To make an impact, investors have to do more than simply create the jobs that a purely financially motivated investor would have generated. They have to create the *additional* jobs, the improved soil, or the extension of green energy that would not have occurred without that motivated investment.

That means understanding what exactly those social and environmental benefits are, and it means finding a way to measure and monitor them, as well as value them. Investors have long known how to compare two companies' financial returns. How to contrast the effect that one company has on the local river to another company's impact on regional gender equality is less clear. Wendy Abt, the founder of a strategic investment advisory firm and former deputy assistant administrator at USAID, has dismissed attempts by impact investors to measure the additionality of their efforts as bad science.

"They count the number of hours children spent exercising, the number of meals delivered, or other metric that is too often loosely based on a complex theory of change with no credible way to verify connections between impacts and a company's actions, products, or receipt of a specific investment," she says. "This is a recipe for disappointment that over time will increase the already pervasive cynicism about 'greenwashing' or 'impact washing.'"[29]

---

[29] Wendy Abt, "Almost Everything You Know About Impact Investing Is Wrong," *Stanford Social Innovation Review,* December 18, 2018 https://ssir.org/articles/entry/almost_everything_you_know_about_impact_investing_is_wrong

The difficulty of assessing the value of an impact makes engaging in impact investing a complex undertaking—which is why impact investors usually look for easier solutions.

The Two Winding Paths for Impact Investors: Funds and Projects

Investors who want to invest sustainably and who want to feel that their capital is doing more than simply generating financial returns have two options. The simplest is to let someone else do the impact assessment and valuation for them. They can invest in exchange-traded funds that filter out companies with environmental, social or governance issues.

ESG-screened ETFs are now a huge industry. The latest figures from the Global Sustainable Investment Alliance, a collection of membership-based sustainable investment organizations, puts the value of sustainable investing assets at the start of 2018 at $30.7 trillion.[30] A UN report published in 2020 noted that estimates of the size of sustainable finance worldwide ranges from $3 trillion to as much as $31 trillion depending on how the investments are defined and measured.[31] Between 2010 and 2019, the number of ESG-screened funds (including ETFs) more than doubled from 913 to 1,931, the report states, with assets reaching $856 billion. "Although ESG funds only account for less than 2 percent of the total investment fund universe, they have become an important component of sustainable finance, and have channeled much needed funds into a wide range of industries, such as energy, water and transportation, which are critical for sustainable development," the report says.

The problem is that if we use Jasjit Singh's strong definition of impact, ESG-screened funds deliver little, if any, impact at all. It's possible for an investment fund to screen out companies that operate in controversial areas and still end up with a portfolio that is almost identical to a traditional fund.

---

[30] *2018 Global Sustainable Investment Review,* Global Sustainable Investment Alliance, 2018 http://www.gsi-alliance.org/wp-content/uploads/2019/06/GSIR_Review2018F.pdf

[31] UNCTAD, *Leveraging the Potential of ESG ETFs for Sustainable Development*, United Nations, 2020

For example, Blackrock is one of the world's biggest investment banks. It issues a large number of exchange-traded funds called iShares whose low fees have made them popular among retail customers. Some of these iShares are ESG-screened. A fund called SAWD, for example, screens out exposure to controversial weapons, nuclear weapons, tobacco, thermal coal, oil sands, UN Global Compact violators, and civilian firearms. But that doesn't mean the fund is putting money in organic coffee or solar power plants. Its five largest holdings are Microsoft, Apple, Amazon, Facebook, and Johnson & Johnson. In fact, the fund is almost identical to iShares' CSPX fund, which is not ESG-screened but simply tracking the S&P 500:

iShares MSCI World ESG Screened UCITS ETF (SAWD)		iShares Core S&P 500 UCITS ETF (CSPX)	
Holding	Weight (%)	Holding	Weight (%)
MICROSOFT CORP	3.61	MICROSOFT CORP	5.65
APPLE INC	3.59	APPLE INC	5.01
AMAZON COM INC	2.90	AMAZON COM INC	4.26
FACEBOOK CLASS A INC	1.29	FACEBOOK CLASS A INC	1.94
JOHNSON & JOHNSON	1.16	JOHNSON & JOHNSON	1.73
ALPHABET INC CLASS C	1.14	ALPHABET INC CLASS A	1.62
ALPHABET INC CLASS A	1.08	ALPHABET INC CLASS C	1.62
NESTLE SA	0.93	BERKSHIRE HATHAWAY INC CLASS B	1.55
PROCTER & GAMBLE	0.84	PROCTER & GAMBLE	1.26
VISA INC CLASS A	0.82	VISA INC CLASS A	1.22

Table 1. Comparing ESG vs. non-ESG screened ETF

It's clear that there's very little difference between those two funds even though one is ESG-screened, and one isn't. I suspect that a passive investor who chose to put their money in an ESG-screened fund in order to support socially responsible companies, generate an impact, and improve the world, would be very surprised to find that they were getting something that's little different to a fund that tracks a broad index.

The alternative is to get more hands-on. The Global Impact Investing Network (GIIN) is an industry group that promotes impact investing. It works with dedicated impact investment funds such as Big Society Capital and the Rockefeller Foundation to help direct funds to projects that deliver more than financial returns. Those projects include ventures like Guayakí Sustainable Rainforest Products, a company that makes yerba maté tea sourced in Latin American rainforests, and Disha Medical Services, an eye-care center that treats people in India who lack medical access. Rent-to-Own, a company founded in 2008 by Mark Hemsworth and Patrun Chikolwizu, helps rural entrepreneurs in Zambia select assets such as refrigerators and stoves or hammer mills and irrigation pumps for their businesses, providing low-cost distribution, financing, and training.

Compared to the potential tens of trillions of dollars invested "sustainably," the amount that goes directly into this kind of impact investing looks paltry. In April 2019, GIIN estimated that the impact investing market was worth about $502 billion.[32] That's just between 1.7 percent and 16.7 percent of all the assets managed through sustainable investing (depending on the definition). Choosing a fund from a Blackrock website is much simpler than reviewing a small South American tea company or a clinic in an Indian village. GIIN offers two-day, in-person courses for investors as well as online curricula that are aimed at fund managers to help them choose and assess projects, but investors are still faced with the challenge of valuing the impact that the investment promises to bring. Even when you can prove causality, it's not always clear that the impact that an investment produces delivers a valuable benefit—or any benefit at all.

---

[32] *Sizing the Impact Investing Market,* Global Impact Investing Network, 2019 https://thegiin.org/assets/Sizing%20the%20Impact%20 Investing%20Market_webfile.pdf

To Invest for Impact or for Growth?

GIIN, for example, has an entire section on its website dedicated to climate finance. Its climate investment track directs capital toward investments that "support a low-carbon transition, help to prevent future emissions, and contribute to the sequestration of existing atmospheric carbon."[33] Sample companies in its Energy Access Fund include a firm that sells solar lanterns and home systems in Africa and Asia. But you'll struggle to find in any impact investment project funding for nuclear power. As investor and entrepreneur Lars Tvede has pointed out, nuclear reactors are now safe and clean, and new designs for thorium plants could lead to the use of a fuel that can produce enough clean energy for 100,000 years.[34] That's not an area that impact investing is likely to touch even though the positive effect on both the environment and on the cost of energy may be far larger than solar lanterns, according to Lars Tvede.

The same dilemmas apply in other areas. Impact investors often cite organic farming as a preferred, sustainable alternative to conventional farming methods with their monocultures, artificial pesticides, and genetically modified crops. Triodos Investments, for example, an impact investment firm, describes the rapid growth worldwide in organic agriculture and plant-based diets "and aspires to be a catalyzer for these positive developments through lending and investments as well as through thought leadership."[35] But is the direction of organic farming sustainable, and is the effect on the climate positive? Is there a market for more expensive foodstuffs? Does the funding of organic cocoa beans deliver a better impact than an investment in the genetic modification of a locally eaten crop such as cassava or teff so that it can better survive

---

[33] "Energy Access Debt Fund: Climate Investing Track," TheGIIN.org, last accessed September 15, 2020 https://thegiin.org/case-study/energy-access-debt-fund

[34] Lars Tvede, *Supertrends: 50 Things You Need to Know About the Future,* Wiley, 2019

[35] Triodos Bank, *Towards ecologically and socially resilient food and agriculture systems,* Triodos Bank's vision paper on food and agriculture systems, June 2019 https://www.triodos-im.com/binaries/content/assets/tim/shared/joint-position-papers/triodos-bank-fa-vision-paper_final_june-2019.pdf

droughts or locusts? In some parts of the world, the overall effect of organic farming is positive while in other parts of the world the effect is negative because the baseline, including productivity and inputs used in conventional farming, varies widely.

A 2018 study,[36] for example, noted that organic farming typically reduced yields by between 19 and 25 percent. To produce the same amount of food using organic methods would require expanding production into natural habitats not currently under cultivation, reducing biodiversity. Organic farms also use more animal manure as fertilizer. The nitrogen and phosphorus in that manure can leach into rivers and coastal seas just as easily as it does from artificial fertilizers, creating eutrophication—the removal of oxygen from water that leads to blooms of algae. The study notes that while the leaching caused by organic farming is lower per unit of land, it's not lower per unit of output. The researchers conclude that switching to organic farming "is not always beneficial for smallholders and should therefore not be considered a general strategy for poverty reduction."

Similar dilemmas turn up outside the developing world. By late 2019, auto manufacturers had promised to spend some $225 billion developing new electric vehicles.[37] While electric vehicles will use less energy and emit less greenhouse gases over their lifetimes than a conventional car, the production of their batteries also produces more toxic waste and leads to more eutrophication.[38]

---

[36] Eva-Marie Meemken and Matin Qaim, "Organic Agriculture, Food Security, and the Environment," *Annual Review of Resource Economics* 2018 10:1, 39–63 https://www.annualreviews.org/doi/abs/10.1146/annurev-resource-100517-023252

[37] Tim Levin, "All the things carmakers say they'll accomplish with their future electric vehicles between now and 2030," *Business Insider*, January 28, 2020 https://www.businessinsider.com/promises-carmakers-have-made-about-their-future-electric-vehicles-2020-1

[38] P. Girardi, Alessia Gargiulo, Paola Brambilla, "A comparative LCA of an electric vehicle and an internal combustion engine vehicle using the appropriate power mix: the Italian case study," *The International Journal of Life Cycle Assessment* 20(8) · August 2015 https://www.researchgate.net/publication/277949217_A_comparative_LCA_of_an_electric_vehicle_and_an_internal_combustion_engine_vehicle_using_the_appropriate_power_mix_the_Italian_case_study

And there is little point in companies boasting of reducing their emissions of carbon dioxide in their host countries if their goal is achieved by exporting production to other countries. Lars Rebien Sørensen, the former CEO of pharmaceutical firm Novo Nordisk, has set a goal of zero carbon dioxide emissions at all production sites in China, Brazil and Japan, as well as in the company's native Denmark. It's always easier to focus on the local impact and ignore the broader effects of that impact on others, especially when they're negative.

So why are ESG-screened funds growing in popularity and why is "impact investing" the phrase on everyone's lips? The answer is probably that it's just a fad among lots of researchers at the moment. There is a strong trend in the developed world around sustainability, and in complex settings emotional porn plays a large role, especially when it is a political trend. What is important to understand, though, is that if you want to create the biggest possible impact in the world by investing, then allocating your funds where they generate the most marginal impact is a much more important decision than a choice to engage in impact investing.

How To Make an Impact in Africa

My interest in Africa put me in a prime position to participate in opportunities traditionally rated as "impact investments." I didn't take them. Even though I wanted my investments to have a powerful effect on the continent, even though an important motivation behind my decision to invest in Africa was to help local entrepreneurs build the businesses that could transform the region, I didn't seek out those specialist projects that emphasized impact.

That's because I found that "impact investing" often fails to deliver the effect its investors want while ESG-screened funds provide easy options but have little, if any, impact. It's what most retail investors do but in practice, they're often just buying shares in Microsoft and Facebook.

Impact investing may be the buzzword of the moment but it's complex and difficult, with projects whose benefits are at best challenging to measure and are at worst dubious.

The alternative approach, though, is to grapple with some really complex issues. It means identifying the impact you want to have and making sure that that impact really is as positive as you hope and is not accidentally causing damage. It means knowing how to confirm causality and understand how to measure the effect of that impact as well as the venture's financial returns. And even when you can do all of that, the impact is likely to be local rather than regional. Rent-to-Own may be able to help several thousand small entrepreneurs in Zambia but it won't transform Africa.

There is, however, a different kind of investment that does deliver reliably positive impacts on a large scale. That's what I'll talk about in the next chapter.

Chapter Three

Why Digitalization is the Biggest Lever in Developing Sub-Saharan Africa

On December 30, 2007, Kenya's electoral commission declared the incumbent Mwai Kibaki the winner of the country's presidential election. The count had taken three days. The voting had been largely peaceful.

Kibaki's victory, however, was unexpected. In the National Assembly, the opposition Orange Democratic Movement had taken 99 of the 210 seats. A sister party, the Orange Democratic Movement–Kenya, won another sixteen seats. President Kibaki's Party of National Unity won just 43. Senior ministers, including the vice-president, the defence minister, and the foreign minister all lost their seats and yet if the vote count was accurate, voters who had chosen the opposition in the assembly election had voted for the ruling party's candidate in the presidential election. As if that wasn't suspicious enough, returning officers from the country's central highlands had gone missing, together with the voting results. The region is home to the Kikuyu, the tribe which includes President Kibaki. When the vote in the central highlands was finally counted, Kibaki was found to have won 98 percent of the vote—a number just high enough to make up for his losses across the rest of the country.

The opposition declared the count a fraud. Demonstrations turned violent, then descended into ethnic conflict that targeted Kikuyu. In Kiambaa, a village in the west of the country, hundreds of Kikuyu took refuge in the Kenya Assemblies of God church. Members of the rival Kalenjin tribe placed mattresses soaked in paraffin against the windows then set them on fire, burning thirty-five people to death. The bloodshed continued through January and February, taking the lives of an estimated 1,700 people and displacing as many as 300,000.

To control the violence, the government declared curfews that lasted from dusk to dawn. Transportation, including the use of *matatus*, the privately-owned minibuses that many Kenyans use to travel to work and between cities, was restricted. But that lockdown didn't just stop the movement of people; it also blocked the movement of money. People who had migrated to the cities for work would use the *matutus* to return home and bring cash to their families, or they would trust a bus driver to transport their funds for them. The *matutus* were an informal but vital part of Kenya's financial system. With the minibuses grounded, people in the country couldn't send financial help to relatives trapped in cities. People in the cities couldn't get aid to rural friends and family members displaced by the fighting.

Kenyans soon turned to another way of distributing funds. They started using a mobile payment system that had launched just a few months earlier. M-Pesa (the "M" stands for mobile; "pesa" is Swahili for "money") was the work of Safaricom, Vodafone's Kenyan subsidiary, which had built the system using a grant from the UK's Department for International Development. The initial idea had been to enable entrepreneurs to receive microloans on their phones. What Safaricom found, however, was that the loan's recipients would use the system to send the funds on to other people hundreds of miles away. Safaricom had shone a light one of Kenya's biggest problems: the lack of a financial infrastructure that allowed for the easy transfer of money.

Safaricom redesigned the system it had created for loans to enable anyone to send money between phones. Customers would be able to bring cash to the network's agents. The agents would convert the cash into digital funds on the customer's SIM card, and the customer could then use an SMS message to send the money digitally to a recipient. When the recipient took the message to an M-Pesa agent in their village, they'd receive the transferred funds in cash. The system was crude— it needed to be if it was to work on the cheap Nokia feature phones popular at the time. It was a long way from the QR codes that people in China now scan to pay for everything from a Starbucks Frappuccino to a ride on the Shanghai metro. But it would allow money to flow around a country in which few people owned bank accounts.

Safaricom recruited a network of agents and hoped that the system's usefulness would enable it to spread quickly. The lockdown imposed during the post-election violence gave M-Pesa exactly the push it needed. In the same way that coronavirus quarantines turned Zoom into a household name, so Kenya's curfews made M-Pesa an essential part of the life of much of the country. Soon, millions of Kenyans were placing money on their SIM cards and sending it around a country that was too chaotic for travel.

At the same time, Kenya's own bureaucratic inefficiency gave M-Pesa the freedom to spread. The Department of Finance saw a system built on phone networks as the purview of the Ministry of Information and Communications. The Ministry of Information and Communications regarded M-Pesa as a financial system under the purview of the Department of Finance. Instead of being tied up in red tape and weighed down by taxes, M-Pesa was left free to fill the gap between the ministries and deliver a service for which people had an urgent need. As Herman Singh, a former Vodacom and MTN executive, put it: "You had this amazingly serendipitous event where forces converged to drive out a solution that would have taken decades but took six months."

The impact was widespread. A study found that less than ten years after the launch of M-Pesa, at least one individual in 96 percent of Kenyan households had access to mobile money.[39] Households became more financially resilient. Previously, they would have relied on neighbors and local communities in the event of a crisis, such as a drought or flood. That provided little security if the crisis struck everyone equally. People with access to mobile money knew that they could receive remittances from a much wider network: if the harvest was lower than expected, a relative in town could send them funds.

The growth in financial confidence caused a rise in per capita consumption. That increased consumer demand lifted 194,000 households, 2 percent of the country's total households, out of extreme poverty. The study's researchers estimated that the spread of mobile money had induced 185,000 women to switch from subsistence farming

---

[39] Tavneet Suri and William Jack, "The long-run poverty and gender impacts of mobile money," Science 354 (6317), 1288–1292. December 8, 2016

to business or retail as their main occupation. Fewer people reported working two jobs. More than 167,000 people now work as M-Pesa agents. In 2019, they earned total fees of more than two trillion shillings ($18.7m).[40] Rival networks have developed across the country.

The effect hasn't been felt as widely in other countries. M-Pesa struggled in South Africa and Nigeria, countries with more established banking systems. But in Kenya, the rollout of a single digital solution has had a powerful impact. It's changed people's lives and altered the country. That success needs to be repeated, with more digital solutions applied to the region's various problems.

Why Sub-Saharan Africa Needs Digitalization

The challenge that Kenyans once encountered when they tried to send funds to relatives, friends, or suppliers across the country was huge. The lack of a financial infrastructure held the country back, increased insecurity, and reduced consumption. But Kenya, and the rest of sub-Saharan Africa, is still plagued by similar challenges both large and small. They affect much of life in the region, providing room for corruption, weakening trust, and limiting opportunity.

It's something that I've encountered again and again throughout my time on the continent, in ways big and small. When I first arrived in Kenya, for example, I needed a work permit. Like any government application, and especially a government application in Africa, the permit demands a lot of paperwork. The Department of Immigration Services provides a long list of requirements that depend on the kind of permit you'll need and the kind of work you plan to do. The Application for Permit Class G (specific trade, business or consultancy (KEP/G)), for example, demands articles of association, a shareholding certificate, signed current audited accounts, proof of offshore transaction receipt, and proof of capital to be invested of at least $100,000. The demands for each kind of work permit are burdensome. Piles of forms have to be printed and submitted on paper. Once your permit has been approved,

---

[40] Safaricom Annual Report 2019 https://www.safaricom.co.ke/annualreport_2019/assets/Safaricom_FY19_Financial_Statements.pdf

you can pay the fee with cash, M-Pesa or by credit card. It's not cheap. Kenyan work permits can cost as much as $2,000, so I paid with my Mastercard as I would have done in Europe. The application status switched to "paid," I received a receipt, and I drove to the Immigration Office to have the permit endorsed in my passport.

"Have you paid for the permit?" the immigration officer asked me at the desk.

"Of course," I told him. "I paid with my credit card."

"Then I need you to cancel the payment," he said. "You will have to pay with M-Pesa."

"But I've already paid," I pointed out.

"We cannot accept that payment," the immigration officer insisted. "You need to cancel your payment and pay again, with digital money."

The problem was that the immigration officer had so little faith that his department's own payment system would deliver the fee that he wouldn't accept a credit card payment. We negotiated. In the end, to obtain my permit, I had to print a receipt from my Mastercard statement and bring him the hard copy. He accepted it without further questions or internal checks…pushed my thumb into real ink to leave my fingerprints on a sheet of paper.

It was my first introduction to the unnecessary roadblocks that a lack of a transparent, efficient, digital process throws up. This one wasn't a big roadblock, and it was more amusing than irritating. (At least to me with my inky fingers, although spending four hours in traffic to return to my office to print an unstamped copy of my Mastercard statement wasn't the best use of a morning.) Once I began building businesses in the region, though, I also came across other examples of small inefficiencies and corruption that could only survive in a context that lacks the transparency that digitalization can bring.

One of my employees, for example, had a wife who worked for a travel agency which booked overseas flights for workers at government institutions. The agency would charge as much as 50 percent more than the institution could have paid if it had booked its flights directly from the airline's website. The agency justified its exorbitant mark-up by arguing that the government needed payment credit, which raised the cost of the transaction. In fact, the agency would simply choose the cheapest ticket category and charge for the most expensive. No one at the institution would think to ask for records to make sure that it was paying a fair price and there was no process in place to track payments and ensure fair pricing.

Again, it's a small example of how a lack of digitalization removes transparency and provides room for the kind of shady dealing that afflicts so much of Africa. It makes obtaining a work permit harder. It enables private travel agencies to overcharge government institutions. And, of course, it allows officials to pad their own wallets. Customs officers frequently try to double or triple the value of the goods that my company BeautyClick imports, increasing the amount of customs the company would have to pay. For a small fee, of course, they would be happy to provide a lower and correct valuation. Scrupulous companies like BeautyClick are forced to either pay the extra customs, then compete with rivals who have lower customs expenses and happier customs officials, or look for local materials.

The lack of transparency caused by the absence of a digital trail doesn't just harm small, growing businesses though. It can also have an important effect on the region's economy and its governance.

At the height of the coronavirus pandemic, *The Economist*[41] noted that the gravediggers in the northern Nigerian town of Kano were busier than usual, but no one knew whether or how many of their new clients were victims of Covid-19. No one had checked or counted. The newspaper also pointed out that the World Bank's latest count of the world's poor had excluded sub-Saharan Africa—the world's poorest region—because too few sub-Saharan countries had released credible data. Africa has too few statistics to track progress on 60 percent of the UN's Sustainable Development Goals, and about half of the data it does have are estimates rather than accurate counts. In health clinics, the newspaper says, doctors tend to write patient notes by hand, creating paper records that are ignored and are hard to mine for epidemiological information.

---

[41] "Lacking data, many African governments make policy in the dark," *The Economist*, May 7, 2020 https://www.economist.com/middle-east-and-africa/2020/05/07/lacking-data-many-african-governments-make-policy-in-the-dark

It's difficult to make policy when you're not collecting data or sharing it in a usable form, so decision-makers in Africa are left to make plans in the dark. Without traffic data, African governments can't decide the best places to build new roads. Without access to patient data, they struggle to track and stop diseases. Without accurate census data that can be shared across departments, they can't decide where they need to put new schools and hospitals. Without a reliable and accurate land registry, farmers can't prove ownership, prevent land seizures, or borrow to invest using their property as collateral.

Sometimes, it doesn't take much digitalization to have a big impact. Not every digitalization project has to cover every corner of a country and require a national lockdown to spread virally. A project focused on a particular group or on a single large employer can also have a rapid and powerful effect. In 2007, Nigeria introduced an Integrated Payroll and Personnel Information System (IPPIS), a kind of digital identification system for the country's federal government employees. IPPIS wasn't a national ID card scheme like India's giant Aadhaar system. It only covered a few hundred thousand people who work for the federal government. They needed to register online, print some documents, and provide some biometric data. Even that small requirement met resistance. The Academic Staff Union of Universities threatened to strike, arguing that the system violated the autonomy of universities and the peculiarities of academia, such as sabbaticals and outsourced services. But the rollout continued, requiring employees of the country's armed forces, judiciary and government to register in order to receive their pay.

A series of studies over the next four years found that enrolling government workers into IPPIS's digital ID scheme had removed some 62,000 ghost workers from the government's payrolls. It was saving $1 billion annually and produced a return of 20,000 percent within one year.[42]

---

[42] *World Development Report: Digital Dividends,* World Bank Group, 2016

How Digitalization is Already Transforming Africa

The success of networks like M-Pesa and projects like IPPIS have demonstrated the value that digitalization can bring: its ability to open opportunities, remove constraints, and reduce corruption. Over the last few years, both governments and private companies have attempted, in various ways, to use digitalization to improve governance and business.

One of the biggest issues facing African countries, for example, is its narrow tax base. In 2018, the latest year for which figures are available, France's tax-to-GDP ratio was the highest among OECD countries at 46.1 percent. Denmark's was the second highest at 44.9 percent.[43] As a whole, the OECD's tax-to-GDP ratio averaged 34.2 percent. A 2019 review found that the average unweighted tax-to-GDP ratio of 26 African countries was just 17.2 percent. Nigeria collected just 5.7 percent of its GDP. Only four countries—Morocco, Seychelles, South Africa, and Tunisia—managed to collect more than 22 percent.[44] And these ratios are based on official GDP figures. The large size of the informal economy in most African countries means that those GDP figures are underestimated; real tax-to-GDP ratios will be even lower than reported.

It would be nice to believe that this low tax rate is a deliberate government policy, a belief that low taxation is essential for a growing economy. But it has a lot more to do with the ease with which earners are able to hide their income in sub-Saharan Africa. Low earners don't declare, and high earners have a myriad of ways to channel their cash abroad, launder their incomes, and hide their assets. Especially, hiding the assets abroad means there is no multiplier effect on the African economy. Instead of everyone with an income contributing at a rate they can afford, sub-Saharan African countries come to depend increasingly on the tax revenues of a small slice of the population motivated to pay

---

[43] *Revenue Statistics 2019: Tax revenue trends in the OECD,* OECD, 2019 https://www.oecd.org/tax/tax-policy/revenue-statistics-highlights-brochure.pdf

[44] *Revenue Statistics in Africa 1990–2017/Statistiques des recettes publiques en Afrique 1990–2017,* OECD/ATAF /AUC 2019

their share, incapable of dodging what they owe, or obliged to declare something even if they don't declare it all. In 2019, fewer than three million South Africans, out of a population of 56 million, paid 97 percent of the country's income tax.[45] In the United States, it takes half of all taxpayers to reach a similar share of federal income tax—more than 70 million people out of a population of 325 million.[46]

Some countries respond by taxing that small, paying portion more heavily, increasing the incentive to hide wealth and creating a vicious circle. South Africa's top rate of income tax has recently crept up from 40 percent to 45 percent. Other countries, though, continue to hold down the top rate of tax. Kenya's top rate kicks in for all income over just 564,709 KES ($5,275). That rate is still only 30 percent.

A better solution is to ensure that everyone eligible to pay income tax is registered, their income tracked, and that the taxes are easy to pay. In October 2014, following the success of M-Pesa, the Kenya Revenue Authority (KRA) launched its KRA M-Service platform, a mobile phone-based tax payment system. Taxpayers could use M-Pesa and the rival Airtel Money platform to make tax payments of up to 140,000 shillings a day using their mobile phones. The following year, as part of its Revenue Administration Reforms and Modernization Program, KRA launched iTax, a more sophisticated Web-based system that the government hoped would simplify both tax registration and collection. Kenyan taxpayers could enter their tax registration details, upload their returns using Microsoft Excel or Open Office, register their tax payments, make status enquiries, and apply for a tax compliance certificate. The system could be used for declaring employment income, business income, and rental income, as well as for filing VAT, and the PAYE and Standards levy for the Kenyan Bureau of Standards. The system also enables the government to identify defaulters, issue reminders, and calculate fines

---

[45] Adriaan Kruger, "SA's problem of a narrow tax base and high taxes," *MoneyWeb,* January 8, 2020, https://www.moneyweb.co.za/news/south-africa/sas-problem-of-a-narrow-tax-base-and-high-taxes/

[46] Erica York, "Summary of the Latest Federal Income Tax Data, 2020 Update," *TaxFoundation.org*, https://taxfoundation.org/publications/latest-federal-income-tax-data/

Digital Africa

and interest for late payments. It's not all good news for taxpayers, who prefer to keep individual payments low.

A 2017 study by researchers at the IMF found that use of the digital tax platform grew rapidly through to the second quarter of 2016.[47]

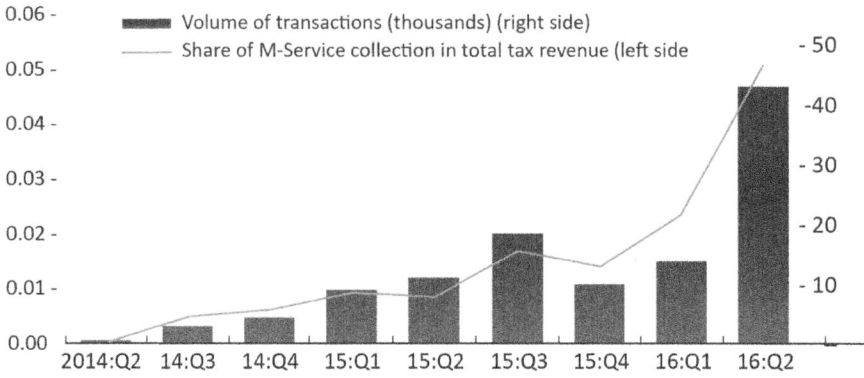

Figure 5. Kenya tax remittances through KRA M-Service
(Digital Revolutions in Public Finance)

The researchers were optimistic about the prospects for better tax payments. They expected that even businesses in the informal economy would soon be able to participate in formal financial transactions and pay their taxes electronically. "With time, these formal transactions will translate to formalization of the businesses themselves," they predicted.

In the meantime, tax returns as defined by the IMF have increased. The tax-to-GDP ratio grew from 19.1 percent in financial year 2013/2014 to 20.3 percent in financial year 2015/2016.

---

[47] Sanjeev Gupta, Michael Keen, Alpa Shah, and Geneviève Verdier, Digital Revolutions in Public Finance, International Monetary Fund, 2017

Why Digitalization is the Biggest Lever in Developing Sub-Saharan Africa

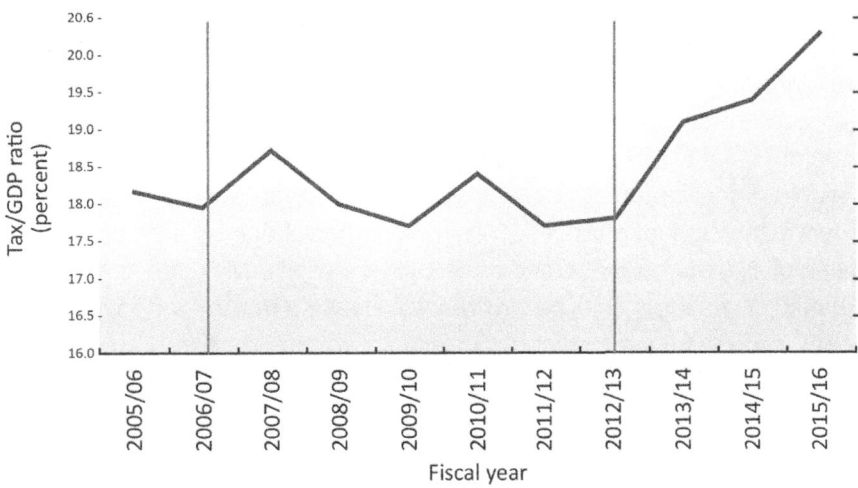

Figure 6. Kenya's tax-to-GDP ratio (Digital Revolutions in Public Finance)

That expansion of the tax base represented an increase in tax revenue of 324 billion shillings between 2011 and 2015 even as the cost of collecting that revenue fell. The perception of corruption among tax officials also declined between 2008 and 2015 from 85 percent to (a still high) 75.8 percent. At the end of June 2019, the KRA reported that more than 3.6 million Kenyans had filed their 2018 tax return, an increase of more than 400,000 taxpayers since the previous year. There were also smaller queues as the deadline approached. KRA attributed the improvement to the efficiency of the iTax platform and the Authority's campaign to encourage the early filing of returns. "The growth in the numbers show positive progress in tax compliance, a move that will eventually drive the country towards economic self-reliance," the KRA said, somewhat hopefully.[48]

It hasn't all been plain sailing. Bugs often hit the iTax platform, preventing taxpayers from logging in. Participants in the informal

---

[48] "More than 3.6 Million Kenyans file returns as deadline closes," Kenya Revenue Authority (Press release), July 1, 2019 https://www.kra.go.ke/en/media-center/press-release/575-more-than-3-6-million-kenyans-file-returns-as-deadline-closes

economy can still avoid registering and paying taxes; Kenya's tax base is still narrow and too dependent on a small percentage of the working population. But digitalization has made filing and paying taxes easier, increased returns, and created opportunities for better governance. It's a major driver in progress towards tax compliance.

And digitalization isn't only helping the Kenyan government to raise revenue through taxation. In 2011, the National Treasury and the Central Bank of Kenya began work on a project called M-Akiba ("Akiba" is Swahili for "savings.")[49] The aim was to release a three-year government bond that retail investors could purchase on their mobile phones using M-Pesa or Airtel Money. The interest rate was 10 percent per year and to encourage take-up, the minimum investment was set as low as 3,000 shillings (around $30). The aim was to enable the government to bypass the banks, which often colluded to force the government to raise yields, and borrow directly from the public. At the time, only 10,000 retail investors held government bonds, making up just 2 percent of bond owners. M-Akiba was aiming at a market of 30 million people with mobile money accounts. Retail investors would get a higher rate of return for their savings. The government wouldn't be forced to raise yields to satisfy a cartel of banks. Everyone would have a chance to lend to the government.

In March 2017, M-Akiba launched a three-week pilot worth 150 million shillings. Just over 100,000 people registered, and the entire bond sold out to 5,692 investors. Three months later, the official launch offered a billion shillings worth of bonds.

The result this time was disappointing. Although more than 300,000 people registered, only 5,988 investors made a purchase. Less than a quarter of the total bonds available sold, even after the government extended the purchase period.

There were a number of reasons that the sale failed to meet expectations. The offer took place during national elections when

---

[49] Tamara Cook and Evans Osano, "The Story of M-Akiba: Selling Kenyan treasury bonds via mobile," *FSD Kenya* (blog), May 10, 2018 https://fsdkenya.org/blog/the-story-of-m-akiba-selling-kenyan-treasury-bonds-via-mobile/

political coverage swamped media advertising. New regulations had forced banks to raise their own interest rates on savings from zero to 7 percent, increasing competition for savings. Registrants were also confused by the product and by the purchase process, with many potential investors not realizing that their purchase wasn't complete.

And yet, despite those teething problems, 85 percent of buyers had never bought a bond before, and 84 percent said that they would recommend the process to someone else. Digitalization has given the Kenyan government a new way to borrow money, and given Kenyans a new and convenient way to invest.

It's not only governments who are making impacts with digitalization though. If you include related sectors, as much as half of Kenya's GDP depends on agriculture. More than three-quarters of the population still makes at least some of their living from farming but the sector has suffered from fragmentation, inefficiency, and a lack of information. Distribution in Kenya was disorganized. Farmers struggled to get their crops to wholesalers and find the best prices. Retailers couldn't always obtain deliveries. The inefficiencies in distribution meant that much as 30 percent of the harvest was lost before it could reach consumers. In 2014, entrepreneurs Peter Njonjo and Grant Brooke developed Twiga Foods, a new kind of distribution network that used digitalization to match growers with vendors, and enabled rapid and convenient payments.

Farmers use a mobile phone app to register their accounts. When they deliver their goods to a local Twiga collection center, they receive a digital receipt and are paid using M-Pesa within 24 hours. Twiga then moves the goods through its warehouses and processing centers. Vendors can place orders using the company's USSD platform, an SMS-like messaging system that works on feature phones. Twiga delivers the products to the vendors, receiving payment and issuing receipts using mobile phones. Farmers have a reliable market for their goods. Vendors have an easy way to source their products. All parties can use digital technology to make their transactions, and waste is reduced, lowering prices for consumers.

The company is still growing. In October 2019, Twiga announced that it had raised a total of $30 million from lenders and investors led by Goldman Sachs. Some 17,000 farmers and 8,000 vendors had registered on the network. Post-harvest waste for farmers and vendors on Twiga is as low as 4 percent, saving customers money and creating new opportunities for increased consumption.

"If you're spending 55 percent of disposable income on food, if that number were to go down to 40 percent—because of...gaining efficiency—what you've done is to release 15 percent for consumers to spend for other things," Peter Njonjo told *Techcrunch* in 2019.[50]

Twiga is now outgrowing the agricultural sector. Only about half its business is now fruits and vegetables with the other half expanding to fast-moving consumer goods. Its new investment will help the company to grow across West Africa and may open new opportunities in ecommerce.

By applying a digital solution to Kenya's broken distribution system, Twiga has created new efficiencies, higher revenues for farmers and sellers, and new opportunities for more business.

Similar projects are growing across Africa. In Nigeria, Kitovu invites farmers to send in their GPS co-ordinates to receive a soil analysis and fertilizer recommendations. The company's mobile platform links farmers with manufacturers, produce buyers, and input buyers, enhancing traceability. Flutterwave, a fintech company based in San Francisco and Lagos, raised $35 billion in a Series B round at the start of 2020. The company already operates in ten African countries, enabling 86,000 small, medium, and large businesses to send and receive payments. Customers include Uber, Booking.com, and Jumia, as well as individuals who use Flutterwave's point of sale technology in the same way that US sellers use Square. In 2019, Flutterwave integrated the payments for pop star Cardi B's performances in Nigeria and Ghana. In the same year, the company, which was only founded in 2016, processed 107 million transactions worth a total of $5.4 billion.

In Ethiopia, Dr. Wuleta Lemma, a US-educated doctor, is turning the old practice of keeping analog health records into a new digital

---

[50] Jake Bright, "Kenya's Twiga Foods eyes West Africa after $30M raise led by Goldman," Techcrunch, October 28, 2019 https://techcrunch.com/2019/10/28/kenyas-twiga-foods-eyes-west-africa-after-30m-raise-led-by-goldman/

practice. Working with Tulane University Centre for Global Health Equity and Microsoft's 4Afrika initiative, her Health Management Information and Disease surveillance system provides an analytics dashboard that gives health administrators real-time access to health data. Dr. Lemma's Tenacare system is now used in 3,000 facilities across Ethiopia, where it processes more than 150 million healthcare records.

These are the kind of impacts that can transform the continent, and they're happening through digitalization.

Digitalization Is Only Beginning in Sub-Saharan Africa

What each of these examples shows is the potential impact that digitalization can bring to sub-Saharan Africa. It's an impact far more powerful than investing in an ESG-screened fund can deliver, and it's an impact with a much wider effect than, for example, investing in a fairtrade coffee plantation or an organic farm with potentially dubious benefits. It's investments like these that are changing the region and pulling Africa into a new period. They're increasing financial security, broadening the tax base, and making markets more efficient. They're helping farmers reduce waste, find buyers, and improve their harvests. They're making it easier for small sellers—as well as large companies—to take payments and issue receipts, which in turn makes it harder to avoid taxes. And they're improving healthcare outcomes by turning paper records into mineable data.

They're increasing consumption and they're growing new opportunities. They're making sub-Saharan Africa more prosperous.

But there's still a lot to do. The large impacts that these digitalization projects have generated show not just the transformative power that digitalization can bring to bear, but also the size of the inefficiencies that remain in African markets. Twiga Foods' reduction of agricultural waste is an important step in boosting efficiency in Kenya's most important sector, and it promises further improvements across the region and across different industries. But Kenya's distribution networks are still a long way from the efficient farm to supermarket channels that characterize food deliveries in Europe or the United States. The Kenyan government is still collecting too little income tax from too few people—and leaking too much of what it does try to collect along the way. The relative failure of M-Akiba's second bond offer shows that the impact of digitalization is limited when too few people understand how to make the most of it, or when the technology itself is poorly designed. There is still work to do.

So why isn't more work being done at a much higher pace? Why aren't investors pouring money into start-ups that will digitalize all of Africa's hospitals tomorrow? Why aren't companies creating more ways to help governments track and collect taxes, make smarter decisions, and help small businesses find their markets, deliver their goods, and take payments? Why aren't initiatives like M-Pesa cropping up across the continent at a much quicker speed?

The answer lies in the difficulties of turning digital ideas into real products in sub-Saharan Africa. That's what we'll explore in the next chapter.

Chapter Four

The Tech Investment Eco-System in Sub-Saharan Africa

Digitalization is changing Africa. Thanks to the development of M-Pesa and other mobile money services, funds can now reach anyone on the continent, anywhere, at any time. Thanks to government-led projects like IPPIS, countries have an opportunity to reduce corruption and save money that they can put to better use funding services. Companies like Twiga and Mdundo have shown that producers can reach and earn from consumers across the country and across borders.

Slowly, sub-Saharan Africa is becoming more connected, more efficient, and more prosperous.

But that change is only coming gradually. South Africa's economy grew by just 0.8 percent in 2018. Nigeria's grew by just 1.9 percent even as its population grew by 2.8 percent. Overall sub-Saharan Africa's growth rate was just 2.4 percent that year, at a time when countries had the opportunity to use digitalization to remove so many of the obstacles holding their economies back.[51]

So why isn't it happening? Why is the story of the digitalization of sub-Saharan Africa a patchwork tale of individual projects instead of the story of the transformation of a continent? Why aren't investors throwing money at African entrepreneurs and their smart tech ideas with the same zeal with which venture capitalists funded Californian start-ups in the late nineties? Why hasn't Africa produced tech giants like China's Alibaba, WeChat, or Huawei?

---

[51] "GDP growth (annual %)," The World Bank, accessed September 15, 2020 https://data.worldbank.org/indicator/NY.GDP.MKTP.KD.ZG

Digital Africa

The problem isn't that African tech start-ups are getting no funding at all. In 2019, African technology companies enjoyed a record year: funding grew by 47 percent compared to 2018. The number of start-ups funded increased by 50 percent. Altogether 311 companies received funding from 261 investors. They shared out $491.6 million, of which $200 million went to Interswitch alone, a billion-dollar Nigerian payment company.[52] As with most data that comes out of Africa, the numbers are questionable, but the figures do give a fair indication of what is happening in the region.

Those figures, though, are dwarfed by the almost $46 billion that flowed into Africa as a whole the previous year according to the UNCTAD.[53] That money wasn't running towards start-ups that were building digital ventures with the power to change the continent. It was going where money has always gone in Africa—largely into the ground, to mining, quarrying, manufacturing, and construction.

Table 2a. Net cross-border M&As by industry, 2017-2018 (Millions of dollars)

Secondary/industry	Sales		Purchases	
	2017	2018	2017	2018
Total	3 452	1 570	1 987	3 651
Primary	30	-59	2 136	205
Mailing, quarrying and petroleum	30	-59	2 136	205
Manufacturing	284	-247	316	-67
Food, beverages and tobacco	9	426	55	-73
Coke and refined petroleum products	-	-973	-10	-
Motor vehicles and other transport equipment	-	215	-	-
Services	3 137	1 876	-485	3 513
Trade	80	-	383	-253
Accommodation and food service activities	45	-50	26	-
Information and communication	-373	37	-5 254	497
Financial and insurance activities	506	1 615	3 542	2 970
Business activities	2 699	215	231	274

---

[52] Disrupt Africa, *African Tech Startups Funding Report 2019*, https://disrupt-africa.com/funding-report/
[53] UCNTAD, *World Investment Report 2019: Special Economic Zones*, 2019 https://unctad.org/en/PublicationsLibrary/wir2019_en.pdf

Table 2b.	Announced greenfield FDI projects by industry, 2017-2018 (Millions of dollars)			
Secondary/industry	Africa as destination		Africa as investor	
	2017	2018	2017	2018
Total	83 044	75 722	5 278	8 579
Primary	10 587	16 795	-	2
Mailing, quarrying and petroleum	10 587	16 795	-	2
Manufacturing	20 583	32 996	2 864	2 890
Food, beverages and tobacco	6 175	11 006	1 229	1 128
Coke and refined petroleum products	1 472	6 480	9	-
Motor vehicles and other transport equipment	1 990	4 982	124	65
Metals and metal products	1 078	3 919	-	195
Services	51 874	25 932	2 414	5 687
Business service	2 539	5 291	680	1 306
Construction	5 667	4 789	192	1 420
Electricity, gas and water	37 073	5 697	29	969
Transport, storage and communication	3 656	4 243	444	342

Tables 2a and b. Net cross-border M&As and announced greenfield FDI projects in Africa by industry, 2017-2018 (Source: UNCTAD)

"Growing demand for and prices of some commodities, as well as sustained non-resource-seeking investments in a few countries, were largely responsible for the higher FDI flows to the continent," said the UN. Very little was going to non-resource-seeking investments in digital industries.

Despite the huge opportunity for investors and for the population of sub-Saharan Africa to profit from the tech start-ups that Africa needs, investors remain largely wedded to traditional investment targets. They still want to earn from mining, building, manufacturing, and infrastructure. It's a missed opportunity that's holding back the continent—and it's caused by the conditions in which African technology companies have to grow.

How Governments Create the Conditions for Digitalization

The half-a-billion dollars of tech funding that African ventures received in 2019 works out at less than 50 cents for each citizen. The same year, just north of Africa, the start-ups of a country with a population of less than ten million received sixteen times Africa's total tech investment. The $8.29 billion of investment funds that Israeli technology firms received was shared among 522 companies, almost double the number of companies that won funding across all of Africa. The digital innovations that Israel has produced haven't just transformed the country from a place of orange orchards and collective farms into the Start-Up Nation. They've also transformed the world. China's WeChat platform began life as a clone of Israel's ICQ messaging system. Israeli innovation has re-designed Intel's chips. Waze, now owned by Google, set a new standard in real-time mapping and traffic updates. Mobileye, which Intel bought for $15.3 billion in 2017, is a world leader in autonomous driving technology and is fitted into cars made by BMW, Audi, Volkswagen, Nissan, Honda, and General Motors, among others.

Researchers have cited numerous reasons for Israel's ability to attract so much venture capital (and successfully transform that capital into valuable products), including a culture that disdains hierarchies, rewards risk-taking, and encourages independent decision-making. In *Start-Up Nation: The Story of Israel's Economic Miracle*,[54] Dan Senor and Saul Singer focus on two particular characteristics that make the country a magnet for VC funds.

The first is immigration. Between 2010 and 2019, more than 255,000 immigrants arrived in Israel, over half of them from the countries of the former Soviet Union, many with advanced degrees. Around ninety percent of the country's population are immigrants, descendants of immigrants or the grandchildren of immigrants. The authors suggest that people who are willing to move from one country to another are natural risk-takers and they describe a country made up of immigrants and their immediate descendants as a nation of entrepreneurs.

---

[54] Dan Senor and Saul Singer, *Start-up Nation: The Story of Israel's Economic Miracle*, Twelve, 2009

The Tech Investment Eco-System in Sub-Saharan Africa

A similar dynamic has powered America's Silicon Valley. Sixty percent of STEM (science, technology, engineering, or mathematics) workers with at least a bachelor's degree in the Bay Area are foreign-born.[55] American billion-dollar tech firms with at least one immigrant co-founder include Google, Tesla, Uber, and Palantir. Immigrant chief executives now lead Microsoft, Google, and Palo Alto Networks. Governments that provide a welcome mat for foreign-born talent and give them the space to develop, give their digital economies the skills, the leadership, and the vision they need to succeed.

Israel, though, also has its own government-managed incubator. The country enforces national conscription at the age of eighteen for both men and women, with men serving as long as two-and-a-half years. Before conscription, the Israel Defence Forces scout schools for high-performing pupils, encouraging them to join its elite cyber programs. Recruits to its Talpiot program agree to remain in the military for at least nine years. They complete a degree in physics, computers, or mathematics, and serve as officers in a variety of military positions. Alumni include Uri Rokni, a neuroscientist at Mobileye, and Avi Loeb, now a theoretical physicist at Harvard University. It was Talpiot graduates who founded XIV, a data storage company sold to IBM in 2008 for $400 million. Marius Nacht, a co-founder of Check Point, a cyber-security firm now worth $16 billion, is also a graduate of Talpiot.

Check Point's other co-founders, Gil Shwed and Shlomo Kramer, completed their service in Intelligence Corps Unit 8200, Israel's cyberwarfare section. That unit doesn't just protect the country's digital infrastructure (and occasionally distribute viruses that attack the infrastructure of enemy countries). It also acts as a conveyor belt, guiding tech-minded recruits through training, work, and leadership, and out into Israel's start-up scene. Alumni have founded companies including Wix, Radware, Palo Alto Networks, and NICE Systems.

"What's interesting is that the experiences of young guys in the army during their military service prepare them for a large extent for the world of startups, innovation, and entrepreneurship almost better

---

[55] *Silicon Valley Competitiveness and Innovation Project - 2019 Update,* Silicon Valley Leadership Group, Silicon Valley Community Foundation, SVCIP.com, 2019 https://www.svcip.com/files/SVCIP_2019.pdf

than any institution of higher learning or any other method," Brig. Gen. (res.) Nadav Zafrir, the unit's former commander told newspaper *Globes* in 2017.[56]

Recruitment to Unit 8200 is highly selective, and includes sociometric tests, psychological tests, personal interviews, leadership tests, tests of cooperation, and the ability to adapt and learn quickly. By the time the recruits have completed their service in the unit, not only will they have learned new skills and implemented them under pressure, they will also have bonded and networked. Alumni leave with access to a network of investors and advisors who have been through the same system and know that the entrepreneurs they're listening to have already been assessed and trained. Glilot Capital Ventures, for example, is a VC firm led by two alumni of Unit 8200 that specializes in investing in other companies founded by the unit's graduates. Six of its first eight portfolio companies have achieved a successful exit. Brig. Gen. (res.) Nadav Zafrir himself left the military in 2013 and set up Team8, a venture capital fund and incubator. In June 2020, the company raised $104 million for a new venture capital arm for start-ups working on data, artificial intelligence, cybersecurity, and enterprise technologies.

Few countries have the same need for a cyberwarfare unit with government-funded selection and training. But other countries have found ways to identify and raise talent, and build the environment in which digital start-ups can flourish. Like Israel, Singapore is a small country with limited natural resources that has also managed to build a thriving technology industry. It's done that in part by building an advanced IT infrastructure. Broadband speeds in Singapore are the fastest in the world, reaching nearly 200 Mbps according to Speedtest, more than double the global average. (The fastest African country is South Africa with 33.14 Mbps, followed by Ghana with 32.98 Mbps.) The country has also had a liberal immigration policy that encourages foreign talent to take residency. A number of different government organizations have overseen immigration over the years, including CONTACT SINGAPORE,

---

[56] Tali Tsipori, "8200 graduates aren't like 23 year-olds in Texas or Norway," Globes, June 5, 2017 https://en.globes.co.il/en/article-8200-graduates-are-not-like-23-year-olds-in-texas-or-norway-1001191294

The Singapore Talent Recruitment (STAR) Committee, and Manpower 21. Each has aimed to balance Singapore's low fertility rate with educated immigrants, often from India, China, Malaysia, and Indonesia. The Global Talent Competitiveness Index 2020 collected in part by INSEAD, put Singapore third, behind only Switzerland and the United States.[57] (Mauritius is the highest ranked sub-Saharan country; it's placed at 49th on the list, out of 132 countries.)

S. Iswaran, Singapore's Minster for Communications and Information, has identified what he calls the "enabling conditions" that give room for local technology companies to grow.[58] The country is politically stable, he says, gives strong legal protections to intellectual property, and has an educated workforce. More than 37 percent of Singaporean school-leavers enrolled in a publicly funded, full-time degree course in 2018, the last year for which figures are available.[59]

The government also plays an active role in the economy. In 2016, the Singaporean government founded SGInnovate, a publicly-owned organization tasked with helping entrepreneurial scientists build Deep Tech start-ups. The organization acts as both an advisor to Singaporean start-ups and an investor in them. It's made more than 80 investments in local companies, totalling over S$51 million ($36.26 million). It also acts as a manpower service, providing a careers marketplace for employees and start-ups and placing students in Deep Tech start-ups for between three and six months. Its community events bring together experts and community members to share ideas and learn from each other. Singapore's government has also matched VC funds, creating pools of private capital and helping to ensure that local start-ups have the money they need to test their ideas.

---

[57] *The Global Talent Competitiveness Index 2020,* INSEAD, The Addecco Group, Google, 2020 https://www.insead.edu/sites/default/files/assets/dept/globalindices/docs/GTCI-2020-report.pdf

[58] Zen Soo and Chua Kong Ho, "Creating an innovation culture - Singapore's not-so-secret formula to becoming a regional tech hub," *South China Morning Post,* September 7, 2019

[59] Ministry of Education Singapore, *Education Statistics 2019*, Management Information Branch Research and Management Information Division Ministry of Education, October 2019 https://www.moe.gov.sg/about/publications/education-statistics

Singapore's actions are dirigiste. SGInnovate's focus on "Deep Tech" such as artificial intelligence, 5G networks, and data science have an element of the government picking winners, a choice that's usually best left to the market. But Singapore's actions, like Israel's, do help to solve the two biggest issues that stand in the way of the development of digital solutions with the power to change a region: talent and funding.

Both countries also provide independent legal systems and enforceable contracts that ensure legal protection for intellectual property and private assets. Since 1976, Africa has had a body responsible for overseeing intellectual property rights. ARIPO, the African Regional Intellectual Property Organization, has nineteen members and was established "to pool the resources of its member countries in industrial property matters together in order to avoid duplication of financial and human resources."[60] It hasn't been very successful. Between 1984 and 2019, the organization received 11,896 patent applications—89 percent from countries outside Africa. Just 2.5 percent of the patent applications came from ARIPO member states.[61]

Unless it's particularly complex, technology is often hard to protect. It's even harder in sub-Saharan Africa. In practice, a start-up in Africa that produces a good, patentable idea can expect to have limited protection from other businesses copying it or from government departments that want to seize its rewards—unless the company has government involvement. That's not the kind of government support that investors and entrepreneurs tend to look for, and without stronger legal protection that can better enable technology firms to profit from their investments and efforts, sub-Saharan Africa will struggle to attract funding and entrepreneurs.

Rwanda, and further north, Tunisia, are both trying to build the kind of government support found in Israel, Singapore, and China (where Innoway, a government-supported incubator, is responsible for about a third of the country's venture capital investments), but on the whole, African countries do not yet have equivalent solutions.

---

[60] "Our History," ARIPO, last accessed September 15, 2020 https://www.aripo.org/about-us/our-history/

[61] Fernando dos Santos, "ARIPO: promoting innovation in Africa," *WIPO Magazine,* November 2019, https://www.wipo.int/wipo_magazine/en/2019/si/article_0003.html

Digital Talent in Africa

Clearly, there's a big difference between the contexts of two small countries in different parts of the world and the 46 countries of sub-Saharan Africa and their billion-plus population. None of those African countries, for example, has a need for a military cyber-security unit that can also act as talent scout, training program, and networking event for its hi-tech industry.

Some governments are trying to help. Tunisia's Startup Act, passed in 2018, provides corporate tax exemptions for start-ups for up to eight years, exemption from capital gains taxes on investments made in start-ups, special custom rules, and even salaries for up to three founders during the company's first year of operations. It's often touted as a model for other countries to follow. Rwanda's National ICT Plan has laid fiber-optic cables and promoted digital literacy. The country's National Innovation Fund, managed by Angaza Capital, aims to bridge the gap between seed funds of up to $250,000 and traditional growth capital of more than $10 million—exactly the place where start-ups struggle most.

These programs, combined with grass-roots initiatives, are having some effect. A World Bank report published in 2016 found 117 technology hubs across Africa, of which 38 had some form of government or academic involvement.[62] In 2019, a new report, using criteria that included incubators, accelerators, university-based innovation hubs, maker spaces, technology parks, and co-working spaces, counted no fewer than 618 tech hubs, a 40 percent increase on its own count the previous year.[63]

---

[62] Tim Kelly and Rachel Firestone, "How Tech Hubs are helping to Drive Economic Growth in Africa," *Background Paper for the World Development Report 2016: Digital Dividends, 2016,* http://documents.worldbank.org/curated/en/626981468195850883/pdf/102957-WP-Box394845B-PUBLIC-WDR16-BP-How-Tech-Hubs-are-helping-to-Drive-Economic-Growth-in-Africa-Kelly-Firestone.pdf

[63] Dario Giuliani and Sam Ajadi, "618 active tech hubs: The backbone of Africa's tech eco-system," GSMA, July 10, 2019, https://www.gsma.com/mobilefordevelopment/blog/618-active-tech-hubs-the-backbone-of-africas-tech-eco-system/

But the relative weakness of government support means that start-ups in the region are largely left to grapple with the challenges of recruitment and funding alone. They start with a handicap.

Sub-Saharan Africa might have a large and growing young population but only about 9 percent are in any form of tertiary education. Governments are more inclined to spend money on primary and secondary education, where their money will reach more students, including those at the bottom of the pyramid instead of touching only those with the means to reach universities. Colleges in the region are underfunded, with half as many professors per student than the global average, according to a report in *The Economist*.[64] Students are also more likely to study humanities than sciences which are more expensive to teach.

One result is that ambitious students look abroad for their education. Nearly 5 percent of students from sub-Saharan Africa travel overseas for their degrees.[65] Kenya currently has nearly 15,000 students studying abroad, with the largest number going to the United States.[66] Nigeria has more than 85,000 students enrolled outside the country, more than a quarter of them in the United Kingdom and the United States.

Those graduates should help to form a talent pool from which African start-ups can draw. They should also make up the seeds from which new start-ups can grow. The rate of entrepreneurship among new graduates will vary by subject and school, but between 7 and 9 percent of Harvard MBA graduates form a new company as soon as they've completed their degree. At Stanford, the rate can be as high as 18 percent.[67]

---

[64] "A booming population is putting strain on Africa's universities," *The Economist,* August 10, 2019

[65] UNESCO Institute for Statistics http://data.uis.unesco.org/Index.aspx?DataSetCode=EDULIT_DS&popupcustomise=true&lang=en

[66] Global Flow of Tertiary-Level Students, UNESCO, last accessed September 15, 2020 http://uis.unesco.org/en/uis-student-flow

[67] John Byrne, "The Top Startups Launched by M.B.A. Students," *Forbes,* February 28, 2019 https://www.forbes.com/sites/poetsandquants/2019/02/28/the-top-startups-launched-by-mba-students/#4a1158c3137e

For African graduates, the opportunities look very different. Having travelled abroad, many will take the opportunity to remain outside Africa and earn a higher salary than they could make at home. One in nine Africans with a tertiary education lives in an OECD country, says *The Economist*. Even for those who return, as well as for those who graduate locally, the weight of responsibility makes forming companies particularly risky. An African student will be expected not just to take care of themselves on graduation but also to help look after their immediate family. They will have parents, grandparents, siblings and possibly even cousins who will expect help from a college graduate's salary. Graduates are expected to pay their siblings' school fees and their parents' medical expenses. In a region without a social welfare net, a member of the family with an education and a reliable income is often the best guarantor of emergency help and sometimes the only way to pay for necessities.

To set up their own firm might mean higher returns one day but in the short term, it's more likely to mean a lower income, a harder road, and disappointed dependents. Culturally and financially, entrepreneurship is a much harder choice for African graduates to make—and with so few competing graduates, they have attractive alternative options. Bright, well-educated, local employees are in high demand among international firms operating in the region. A graduate from an American or a British university who is willing to return home instead of enjoying a higher standard of living in London or San Francisco can expect a choice of offers that will give them a respectable income, a comfortable life, and the ability to meet their obligations. It's hard to give all of that up in the hope of making more money running their own company, however strong their entrepreneurial spirit might be.

Graduates who do make the choice to form their own businesses will also face the challenge of competing against those big firms when they come to recruit the help they need. Forming a start-up is a risk but so is working for one. It may be exciting but it's also difficult, demanding, and unreliable. Qualified applicants will need a good reason not to take a safe, high-paid job with a multinational or a safe, low-paid job (with the prospect of harvesting bribes) in a government department.

Employers will then struggle to assess anyone they do find, value them, and retain them. One of the biggest challenges that I've found in recruiting staff in sub-Saharan Africa is determining whether the people demanding high salaries are worth the price they ask. Because opportunities and expectations in Africa are often tied to background and family connections, an applicant with weak qualifications might believe that they're worth much more than their true value because they come from a relatively wealthy family. On the other hand, a highly skilled individual who has never had a chance might ask for a low salary because they feel they have few other options.

And even if you can recruit a good team member, there is no guarantee that you will keep them or that they will recognize that they're part of a team working on behalf of a company whose success is their success. As we'll see in the next chapter, loyalty is an issue among African employees, so companies that invest in their staff can't assume that they'll see a return on that investment.

Of course, to some extent, this is true everywhere. A study by Founders Circle, a VC firm, found that the average employee tenure in Silicon Valley is just two years, and even unicorns can expect an attrition rate as high as 25 percent.[68] When Google invests in new graduates, it can't expect a long-term benefit from those investments.

But it can expect at least a short-term benefit from the investments already made in those graduates. Applicants to both established tech companies and start-ups are competitive. According to Google's LinkedIn page, the five universities that deliver the most "newglers" to Google are Berkeley, Stanford, Carnegie Mellon, UCLA, and MIT. Tech firms in the West, including start-ups, are able to hire people who have already been screened for intelligence and ability by some of the world's top universities. Those new employees arrive with certified knowledge so even if the company is only able hold onto many of those graduates for a couple of years, it will start benefitting from their knowledge right away.

---

[68] "In The Front Door, Out The Back: Attrition Challenges At High Growth Startups," FoundersCircle, last accessed September 15, 2020 https://www.founderscircle.com/high-startup-turnover-rate/

While all countries struggle to find, train, and benefit from specialized talent that can build digital solutions, in sub-Saharan Africa that challenge is particularly acute. Primary and secondary education aren't delivering enough people to tertiary education. Universities and colleges are underfunded and overcrowded. The best talent goes abroad where much of it remains, and the graduates that return are quickly snapped up by established firms and offered jobs where they can lead comfortable, well-paid lives. Start-ups in Africa are often left to scrabble around for skilled employees, hope that they have the ability to do the job, and pray that they'll stay long enough to make an impact. Ideas for the digital solutions that can change the continent have little fertile ground in which to grow.

The situation is improving. The last five years have shown a positive trend with the opening of technology hubs, and more well-educated African founders making the jump towards entrepreneurship. But it's happening too slowly and we need to accelerate the trend.

Africa's Missing Venture Capital

Entrepreneurs also lack the fertilizer that makes their businesses grow. Entrepreneurial graduates of Israel's Unit 8200 can tap the resources of earlier alumni who have already made exits or who are now running venture capital firms. Singapore's business-builders can make their pitches to a government willing to deliver matching funds to ideas that fit its vision of the future.

In sub-Saharan Africa, I've found that investors are willing to put seed money into digital projects. Finding the first half-million dollars to get a digital business idea off the ground is never easy but it's doable. The funding is there. It's at the next funding round where start-ups run into trouble.

This is the stage when the company has turned an idea into a product and proved the business model. Now it needs to scale, a stage that typically requires a funding round of between $500,000 and $10 million in order to take the next step, conquer a market, and turn a small business into a giant with the potential to become a unicorn. In sub-Saharan Africa, that funding is missing—and it's missing for a couple of reasons.

First, sub-Saharan Africa still lacks young investors who both understand the potential of digitalization and have the capital to fund it. A graduate of Stanford with an idea for a technology business has access to an entire eco-system of venture capitalists, incubators, and accelerators funded by people who have already built successful businesses. Reid Hoffman co-founded LinkedIn; he is now a partner at Greylock, a veteran VC fund that takes companies from seed funding through series B rounds and beyond. Peter Thiel, a co-founder of PayPal, formed the Founders Fund, an investment firm which closed $3 billion in new capital in February 2020. Marc Andreessen, co-founder of Netscape, formed a venture capital fund with Ben Horowitz, co-founder of enterprise software company Opsware. The company now has $12 billion in assets under management, and has invested in firms including Facebook, Lyft, Pinterest, and Dollar Shave Club. In China, the country's three big tech firms—Baidu, Alibaba, and Tencent—have made investments in half of China's unicorns.

Someone with a good tech idea in either the Bay Area or Beijing knows where they can go to pitch that idea, and receive the funds they need to test it. The money that technology has made returns to build new tech businesses. There are plenty of young Africans in Nairobi and Kinshasa who follow what happens in digital spaces around the world and are excited about what digital projects can do for Africa. But because so few African companies have exited at high valuations, those young digital experts currently lack access to former entrepreneurs with the capital to take them beyond seed funding.

Older local investors who do have the funds that start-ups need to scale are less likely to understand the potential of digital projects. They'll have made their money in hard assets—in real estate or mining—in property they can see and touch and understand. Persuading them that things they can't see, such as data on a server somewhere, could be worth more than a trainload of minerals or an office building filled with rent-paying tenants is a difficult job. They want secure cashflows from the kind of physical assets that have already built their fortunes.

Entrepreneurs who turn to foreign investors have a different problem. DFIs (Direct Foreign Investment Funds) that are willing to invest in sub-Saharan Africa are aware of the country risk. They know the challenges that corruption can pose to a business. They know that unstable governments can create periods of chaos, and they know how to assess the risks of each country in which they operate. The risks of working in South Africa or Kenya are not the same as the risks of funding a business in Gabon or Sierra Leone.

But while many DFIs are mandated to take country risk, they're rarely mandated to take technology or project risk in the way that venture capital funds do. When they assess projects, they tend to view ideas through the lens of what has already worked abroad. But sometimes business models that work in Europe or the United States struggle in Africa's divided markets and poor infrastructure. Jumia pitched itself as an Amazon for Africa—and even designed its website using similar fonts, arrangements, and colour schemes. Co-founded by two French former McKinsey consultants, the company attracted funding from South African telecom MTN, from Millicom, a provider of cable and mobile services in Latin America and Africa, and from German investor Rocket Internet. In 2019, the company listed on the New York Stock Exchange at $14.50 a share, valuing the company at $1.1 billion. Within four days, the share price had jumped to nearly $50, valuing the company at $3.8 billion. By September 1st 2020, the share price was just $9.48 after dipping at $2.15 in March 2020. The company had been crippled by work practices even more toxic than Amazon's famously challenging work conditions, by allegations of exaggerated metrics, and by the high cost of fulfilment in the countries in which it operated. It has since pulled out of a number of markets.

Meanwhile Twiga Foods continues to grow but has no equivalent in the US or Europe, where the kind of digital supply chain solution it offers is more likely to be built in-house by supermarket chains. Foreign investors looking at digital African solutions for African problems need to understand the specific problems in each country, but they also have to understand the risks of those solutions. At the moment, that combined understanding of both country and project risk is rare. It's growing but it's happening much more slowly than it should—and in the meantime African entrepreneurs are struggling to find funding.

The result is serious: the funding gap prevents companies from scaling. Mdundo, despite being able to pitch itself as a kind of Spotify for Africa, was historically largely bootstrapped. The same growth figures in a different region would probably have attracted the funding it needs to enable much faster scaling. The company would probably be two or three times larger than its current size in a different part of the world.

That impeded growth is not necessarily a bad thing. The VC model in the US and Europe often results in overvaluations and an emphasis on growth ahead of profitability. Uber lost $8.5 billion in 2019, the tenth year since it was founded. The company's investors are still subsidising its customers' journeys by more than a dollar for each ride. And yet its market capitalization remains over $62 billion. African investors are far more sceptical of the kinds of high valuations that start-ups in other parts of the world demand on the basis of market domination one day in the future.

But while a focus on profits and accurate valuations makes for a healthier investment environment, it comes at a cost. Start-ups that lack funds to scale struggle to justify paying the high salaries of the most qualified team members available. They hesitate to build expensive organisations that can only be justified by scaling when they don't know if they can find the funding to pay for that growth. You don't start building a high-speed train if you're not certain there's funding available to build the track. (At least, not usually. Kenya's Lake Turkana Wind Power Station, the country's largest private investment, completed the installation of 365 wind turbines in January 2017. For the next two-and-half years, the propellers turned uselessly while the company waited for the government build the electricity line to connect the farm to the grid.)

Of course, without that expensive talent and without those expensive organisations, a company can't explode and show the investor-case that justifies the scaling funds. Africa is creating a self-fulfilling prophecy of weak growth.

How to Fill the Gap Between African Seed Funding and Scaling

African start-ups find themselves in a Catch-22. Without the funding to scale, they can't grow. Without clear growth, they can't attract the funding they need to scale. African governments are unlikely to break that impasse in the way that governments have in Israel and in Singapore although some, particularly Rwanda's, are trying.

But these kinds of initiatives are rare. African governments lack the funds (and often the vision) to invest in digital infrastructure. Rwanda's program is tiny compared to the dedicated efforts of Singapore's government, but it does show the solution that needs to be implemented to open funding and deliver capital to the entrepreneurs who need it.

Rwanda's National Innovation Fund isn't solely financed by the Rwandan government. Investors include financiers, responsible investment funds, and the African Development Bank. It's that development finance that's critical. The role of development funds is to provide financing where market forces consider the risks too high. They go where private markets can't go—which is precisely the place digitalization in Africa needs to develop. M-Pesa started life as a public/private initiative after Vodafone won funds from the Financial Deepening Challenge Fund, a competition run by the British government's Department for International Development (DFID). The inspiration for M-Pesa also came from DFID. In 2002, the department funded research that showed that arranging remittances was one of the most important reasons that people in Botswana, Ghana, and Uganda used their mobile phones. "Telecommunications operators should consider whether they can facilitate wire transfers and other remittances either directly or through teleshop proprietors," the report suggested.[69]

It's likely that private companies would have spotted the opportunity eventually, but it's less likely that foreign funds would have been willing to invest in the infrastructure that M-Pesa needed considering the high risk of failure and the absence of similarly popular services in investor countries. In Germany, only 15 percent of mobile phone users have sent money to other people from their phones.[70] Government development funds, though, exist precisely to take up those risks and build those opportunities.

---

[69] Kevin McKemey, Nigel Scott, David Souter, Thomas Afullo, Richard Kibombo, and O. Sakyi-Dawson, "Innovative Demand Models for Telecommunications Services." *FINAL TECHNICAL REPORT Contract Number R8069*. Department for International Development (DFID), 2003 https://assets.publishing.service.gov.uk/media/57a08d10e5274a27b20015e3/2936_R8069_FinalReport.pdf

[70] *Mobile Payment Report 2019,* PricewaterhouseCoopers, 2019 https://www.pwc.de/de/digitale-transformation/pwc-studie-mobile-payment-2019.pdf

There's no shortage of these development funds. Germany's DEG is nearly 60 years old. Its portfolio is made up of around 700 investments in 79 countries. It has more than 2.1 billion euros invested in Africa alone. Few of those investments, though, are in digital start-ups. Successful projects include a renewable energy plant in South Africa and a Nigerian cream cracker factory. Like many government-funded investments, there is also an emphasis on helping the lender region's own companies. DEG's AfricaConnect service provides debt financing to European companies who want to invest in African markets. That has a value but it's not the same as providing the funds that enable African digital start-ups to scale—and that's where the biggest impact in Africa will potentially come from.

The IFU, Denmark's Investment Fund for Developing Countries, is no longer tied to a Danish interest or to Danish companies, and is free to invest in any enterprise wishing to do business in any of the 150 countries that are eligible. The project must be commercially viable and have a development impact in the host country. IFU and IFU-managed funds have made co-investments of DKK 209 billion ($31.5 billion) in 1,300 companies around the world, of which IFU says it has contributed DKK 23 billion of its own capital.

But it's clear that one important solution to the funding gap in African digitalization is DFIs—development funds that are willing to take on the kind of risk that commercial lenders and venture capital funds are unwilling to accept. For that to happen though, they will need to change. They already understand country risk but they also need to acquire an understanding of project risk. They need to acquire the skill sets that enable them to assess digital projects that are unique to the African environment and that offer specialized solutions to African problems.

Local entrepreneurs too, need to adapt their pitches to the fund offering the financing. Herman Singh, the CEO of Future Advisory, a digital transformation and start-up acceleration firm, and a former deputy chairman of Jumia, emphasizes the distinction between venture capital, corporate venturing, and development funding in Africa. "They take quite different risk appetites," he says, "and the agendas are very different than the development capital guys."

The Tech Investment Eco-System in Sub-Saharan Africa

The United Kingdom's CDC, a 70-year-old development finance institution once known as the "Colonial Development Corporation," for example, has both a financial incentive that demands a return on investment but also an imperative to help uplift Africa. "They feel they're still very hard-nosed about making sure that the numbers make sense, but they would tend to be more open to investments in I.T.-based businesses or digital-based businesses," explains Singh.

Venture capitalists use the same measures that they use anywhere in the world when they assess projects, adds Singh, while corporate ventures are looking for projects that can support their core business. Each kind of investment is looking for a return and for exits, but they each have a slightly different emphasis, so entrepreneurs looking for investment need to understand what each funding source prioritizes.

"I remember doing a pitch to Unilever, for example, for Jumia," recalls Singh, "and it was very much about how to open up routes to market for and getting access to customer information. That's what Unilever was interested in. When I did the pitch to AXA, that was very much around 'how can this help my core business?'"

Singh's pitch to Goldman Sachs focused on the VC fund while the pitch to CDC was about how their investment could uplift society, create employment, and help small businesses.

Some VCs and DFIs are already combining their understanding of project risk and country risk. A number of the VCs operating locally are backed by DFIs. Novastar Ventures, for example, whose investments include healthcare projects, agritech, and furniture brands, has picked up funding from the UK's DFID, the European Investment Bank, the Dutch Good Growth Fund and FMO, the Dutch Development Bank. Over the last couple of years, the French DFI Proparco has started talking more about the tech investments, but until more investors in Africa are able to assess both project and country risk, entrepreneurs will struggle to find the funding they'll need to scale, and they'll have to adapt their pitches to match the fund.

Access to funding is essential to the development of Africa's start-up scene but it's only part of the problem. Building a company in sub-Saharan Africa is not like building a company in Silicon Valley or in Europe. From recruitment through sourcing suppliers to taxation and bureaucracy, I've found a host of unique challenges and obstacles that small businesses need to overcome in order to grow. I'll talk about those experiences in the next chapter.

Chapter Five

Building Successful Businesses in Sub-Saharan Africa: Innovative Ideas and Business Models

In the previous chapter, we looked at the challenges that businesses in sub-Saharan Africa face as they look for funding. We saw how capital in the region continues to flow towards manufacturing, mining, and construction instead of towards the digitalization that can deliver the impact the region needs. We saw too that while development funds can assess country risk, they currently struggle to assess relevant project risk. The result is that entrepreneurs and start-ups can obtain seed funding at the level of an angel investment in the West, but then have to rush towards profitability and self-reliance instead of focusing on scaling because it's so difficult to find capital to finance the next stage of their growth. Of course, there are well-funded growth cases in the eco-system and the trend is positive, but overall the funding landscape still has substantial gaps. Recent debates in the eco-system have centered on the backing of black vs. non-black founders which, in the bigger picture, is a very relevant issue. But for the tech eco-system in sub-Saharan Africa, the impact of attracting more capital to the total sector is, in my opinion, massive. It's the only way to the secure backing of more local entrepreneurs, black and non-black.

Even if those funds were available, though, they'd need to flow somewhere. They'd need to reach the business ideas and models that promise to deliver the kinds of services that the region needs. In this chapter, we're going to look at how to form those business ideas both in theory and in practice in Africa. We'll examine the generation of business ideas and look closely at idea replication, one approach that's used around the world but has particular relevance in sub-Saharan Africa. We'll also look at business models: how to form them and how they need to be adjusted for the African market.

In the next chapter, we'll move on to the next stage and explore what happens when you want to implement those ideas: hiring and training staff; and forming partnerships.

Generating New Business Ideas in Africa and Beyond

For customers, brands can seem to come from nowhere then follow a straight path to a giant market. An inventor somewhere will have had an epiphany. An idea will have come to them in the shower or while they were sitting in traffic. They mull it over, do some research, and talk to their friends until they're sure that no one else has thought of it. They draw up a business plan, show it to investors, and soon they find that they're sitting on a pile of money just big enough for them to hire a great team, build the product, and start to market it. That marketing proves the concept so that all that's left to do is scale, then either sell up to a bigger company or continue expanding around the world.

It's a reassuring thought. It suggests that anyone can build a successful business if they just have the right idea when they reach for the shampoo in the morning.

In practice, it just doesn't happen that way.

Ideas rarely come out of nowhere. They don't suddenly appear but grow out of older concepts that have already been tried and tested. Entrepreneurs exploit the opportunities created by the businesses that came before them. They innovate existing products or technology, identify current unmet market needs, or see a way to sell a similar service slightly differently. Sky.Garden, an African ecommerce company in which I'm an investor and Chairman of the Board, grew out of an idea pioneered by Shopify and is making the most of the opening created in Africa by Jumia's marketing and consumer education. Jumia itself is an idea that made the most of the opportunity created by Amazon's proven business idea. And Jeff Bezos himself could only have had his idea once the Internet created opportunities to offer products and take orders online.

Good business ideas can build on the ideas that came before them but too few entrepreneurs use the knowledge, experience, and learning that other entrepreneurs have wrung out of their failures to find ideas that work. Opportunities grow in the space created by successful businesses, but they can also grow in the space cleared by other entrepreneurs when they tried and failed to build something new.

Business ideas also rarely come into the world alone. Karan Girotra, a professor at Cornell Tech and the Johnson School at Cornell University, together with his colleagues, have looked at the best way to generate and select commercial ideas.[71] They note that when a company develops the branding and identity for a new product, it doesn't pick one idea one time. It develops a process to generate multiple ideas that it can constantly whittle down and test. "Generating the ideas that feed subsequent development processes thus plays a critical role in innovation," Girotra and his colleagues state.

Zocor, a statin that's one of the world's most prescribed medications, took about a decade to develop, and passed through the discovery of about 10,000 new compounds before Merck hit on its winning formula. Google likes to talk about how its "twenty percent time" led to prototypes for Gmail, Google News, and AdSense, but it doesn't talk about the thousands of hours that other developers spent working on ideas that didn't lead anywhere.

And it's not just product ideas that come in groups. Idea generation relies on mass production, then careful filtering across multiple fields. Logo designers will generate dozens of ideas before whittling them down to a handful that they'll present to a client...who will ask them to come back with a dozen more. Product names start with a long list of possibilities that are assessed and reviewed and voted on. According to Girotra, the name of the Xpult, a catapult used in school science classes,

---

[71] K. Girotra, C. Terwiesch, and K.T. Ulrich, K. T., "Idea Generation and the Quality of the Best Idea," *Management Science*, 56 (4), (2010): 591–605. http://dx.doi.org/10.1287/mnsc.1090.1144

Digital Africa

was one of around twenty first considered. The inventors filtered the options down to the best ten, then the best three, before lighting on the final option.

What should be clear is that idea generation itself isn't difficult. Business ideas are a dime a dozen. The challenge is to select, from the large numbers of ideas that can be produced, the best winning idea that *should* be produced.

Companies and entrepreneurs have to build a way to generate multiple ideas and raise the chances that the ideas they consider will include at least one that can go on to become a viable business. They then need to ask what is the best way to assess, filter, and refine those ideas so that they can identify and build that winning proposition.

Inspired by Karan Girotra, I typically recommend that entrepreneurs follow a proven three-step process:

Figure 7.

This is not to substitute a Lean start-up or Pretotyping way of working. Those two great approaches go hand in hand with this three-step process and help you test and refine ideas.

Idea Generation

Companies can mine ideas from two places: from individual inspiration; and from group brainstorming. Entrepreneurs can either try to think up ideas themselves, or they can get together with friends, colleagues or co-founders to toss around concepts and see what sticks.

In general, individual inspiration is better. Studies have found that "free riding," "evaluation apprehension," and "production blocking" restrict the abilities of groups to generate ideas. When some group members find that they are able to benefit from membership of the group without actually contributing to it, they stay silent and let other members contribute more. Other members may worry about a negative reaction to their ideas; in a group setting they're too intimidated to speak up so their good ideas are left unspoken. And groups are often dominated by individuals who hog the spotlight and crowd out other contributors. When only one person can speak at a time, the ideas that could be the most valuable may be held down by the most talkative member of the group. We've all been in meetings like that.

But while researchers have consistently found that individuals can produce more ideas than groups are able to do in the same amount of time, those ideas also need feedback and assessment. They benefit from discussion and from the contribution of other people with different experiences and viewpoints who can point out flaws and add to the idea's strengths.

Girotra and his colleagues conducted an experiment to see which process was more effective: a group process in which everyone worked together to generate new ideas; or a hybrid process that combined individual innovation with group review.

They recruited 44 volunteers from an upper-level product design course at the University of Pennsylvania and divided them into groups of four. They gave some of those groups half an hour to generate ideas together for the student market: either a sports product or a household product. The students wrote each idea they produced on a single sheet of paper, with notes and a 50-word description. At the end of the discussion period, the researchers gave them an additional five minutes to select their five best ideas.

At the same time, the researchers broke up the other groups and gave each member ten minutes to write and rank their own ideas alone. They then put them back into groups and gave them twenty minutes to share and discuss those ideas, and develop new ones. At the end of that session,entered the researchers also gave those groups five minutes to discuss and rank their best ideas.

To judge the business value of each list of ideas the groups produced, the researchers turned to a set of MBA students and they asked other students to rank the likelihood that they would buy the products the groups suggested.

What Girotra and his colleagues found was that the "hybrid" process that combines individual brainstorming with group discussion produces about three times more ideas than the team process could produce alone.

But business ideas aren't judged by quantity: companies would rather have just one outstanding idea than a hundred mediocre ideas. Girotra and his colleagues also found that the hybrid process produced higher quality ideas. Both in terms of business value and purchase intent, the ideas produced by the hybrid process scored higher among MBA students and potential customers than ideas generated by groups alone. Although developing ideas in teams did lead to concepts that built on previous suggestions, those new ideas, say the researchers, were worse on average than the ideas that were first created by individuals working by themselves.

So the best way for businesses to generate new ideas is a hybrid system. Instead of calling the company or a bunch of co-founders together to toss ideas around, individuals should be coming up with ideas alone then meeting together to discuss and rank them so that they can build the best idea together. VCs don't really like one-person founding teams, so the hybrid process should also lead to the formation of a founding team rather than the approval of an individual's concept.

What I've found interesting in a sub-Saharan context is that the variance in the quality of the ideas in a pool also influences the quality of the selected subset of ideas. If you were to select the best idea from two pools with the same size and the same mean quality, on average, the idea selected from the pool with the higher variance will be better.

So how do you create variance within a group of individuals? Looking for individuals with different backgrounds, including education, gender, place of residence, and cultural experience is a good starting point. Giving diverse individuals the space to think for themselves, away from the judgment of colleagues and friends, and away from the chatty production-blockers, will produce more ideas and higher quality ideas.

According to Girotra, however, while team and hybrid structures can produce, compare, and rank ideas, both are poor at assessing the overall quality of those ideas. Idea selection—the next stage in the development of business ideas—requires a different approach.

Idea Selection

Anyone who has ever sat in a pitch meeting will have been struck by the gap between the passion with which a founder can push an idea and the quality of the ideas that people bring to pitch meetings. As the founder is working through their pitch deck and explaining why if only one in five people on the planet buy this product, the company will be worth more than Apple, all you can think is: "But why would *anyone* want to buy vacuum cleaning shoes?" (Japanese automotive firm Denso really did show off a pair of shoes with in-built vacuum cleaners at the Consumer Electronics Show in 2017, evidence that not all business ideas pass through a selection process and not every selection process is effective.)

Giving individuals time to generate ideas alone may be the best way to produce more and higher quality ideas but we're always the worst judge of our own ideas. We can't see their faults and we assume that the market will love our concepts as much as we do.

Bringing the idea to a group within the entrepreneur's social circle and comfort zone starts the process of feedback and selection but that group may have a similar view of the market. Its members may share a similar experience, a similar outlook, and be prone to the kind of groupthink that fails to highlight the problems with products like Google Plus, the search company's failed attempt to build a social platform, or the limitations of Amazon's Fire phone. When a product gets a thumbs-up from a senior executive, it's often easier for everyone else in the company to fall in line than to oppose what they will later say they always knew was a bad idea. It takes a third party, beyond the group, to raise an eyebrow and point out that no one wants to vacuum the floor as they walk.

For entrepreneurs outside Africa producing business ideas for Africa, obtaining feedback from people on the ground in the region—people who know the target audience and understand the context—is crucial. Too many entrepreneurs have failed in the region because they neglected to do a proper segmentation and understand the important customer segments in depth. Wabona, for example, a company enrolled in 88mph's 2013 accelerator program in Cape Town, wanted to stream African movies and television series to local and diaspora customers. In 2020, this sounds obvious, a replication of Netflix focusing on local African content. But in 2013, an in-depth analysis of the speed and cost of data for the target customer segment would probably have indicated heavy challenges. The idea was sound but it couldn't have worked in that environment at that time.

One obstacle that prevents entrepreneurs from receiving the feedback they need is that in general—and not only in Africa—entrepreneurs are too worried about sharing their ideas before launch. Entrepreneurs often approach me thinking that they have the most unique idea, and ask for feedback on some small sub-set of that idea. They don't tell me everything because they're worried that someone will steal their concept. Typically, I tell them three things:

1. In today's world you should be worried if *no one* has thought of doing the same thing. It's possible that you're a genius who has spotted an opportunity that no one else can see, but it's more likely that everyone else has walked away for a good reason you've missed.
2. If the value is in your idea, how do you protect your position after launch when everyone will know about it? The value of feedback is typically much higher than the "risk" of giving up strict confidentiality.
3. Worry less about confidentiality and more about how you create a sustainable competitive advantage. Can patents protect you? Will you have a better business model or a more effective marketing plan, etc.?

An outside entity or a group of people outside your social circle, says Girotra, is often better than judging your idea alone, and innovation is best judged by a diverse crowd of targets, especially the people who will reap the benefit of that innovation. As well as tossing ideas around in an internal corporate group then, companies should also be looking for community feedback.

In his business school classes, Girotra uses the Darwinator to filter ideas, a Web-based tournament tool that lets companies post suggestions that others can vote on. The entrepreneurial world has similar free online voting tools. As the least popular ideas are winnowed out, the most popular ideas move to the next round until only the winning idea is left. Workshops can work in a similar way, using external evaluators made up of potential users to identify the flaws in ideas.

Companies also assess ideas based on "Real-Win-Worth-it" criteria, a system used by firms as large as 3M, Honeywell, and Novartis. The companies rate ideas based on whether they: meet a real need that customers will be willing to pay to satisfy; bring a competitive edge or a sustainable advantage that will enable the company to lead in the market; and deliver high enough returns to justify the company's effort.

"Real-Win-Worth-it" criteria provide an objective filter through which groups can pass the large number of ideas generated by individuals until the best idea is identified. The filter helps to ensure that business ideas have metrics by which they can be judged before decision-makers choose to devote capital and assets to their production.

The same filter works with entrepreneurial ideas because the same principles apply to all business ideas: they're only worth creating if they meet a real need, deliver a competitive advantage once the idea is out, and can produce rewards big enough to justify the expense and the effort invested in building them.

Of course, the process isn't perfect. Good ideas are sometimes rejected—and many of them will pop up again later, produced by a different firm. Corporate groups, judges, and focus groups sometimes score ideas highly that later fail to find a market. No internal selection process can ever replicate the market entirely and there's always a gap between the idea presented in a pitch meeting and the product that eventually reaches that market. That's particularly true in sub-Saharan Africa, where entrepreneurs are bringing ideas to a context with unique characteristics and a market that might not have seen them before. Sometimes, the reaction of those markets will be surprisingly positive. M-Pesa became so much more than its original vision of a loan distribution channel. But sometimes, it will also be negative. Jumia struggled to build an ecommerce platform in an environment that was still distrustful about buying online and had too few customers plugged into the service. The concept of pretotyping, of making sure you're building the right thing before you build it right, is very valid when testing and refining ideas.

Ideas everywhere—but especially in sub-Saharan Africa—need production and careful management. They'll also need refinement.

Idea Refinement

The process from individual brainstorming to group discussion through workshops and contests is rarely short. It takes time to organize and implement, to find focus groups and gather feedback, to prepare the pitches, vote on ideas, and assess each idea based on "Real-Win-Worth-it" criteria.

And it doesn't end when the entrepreneur has managed to identify the best idea that that hybrid process has generated. The third stage in the process is refinement. Just as no plan ever survives contact with the enemy, so few business ideas are unscathed by contact with the market—starting with angel investors who often have their own suggestions about how the idea should be implemented.

The entrepreneurs don't have to implement those suggestions if they don't want to, of course, but the prospect of receiving funds (and the experience that investors bring to a project) mean that the refinement of an idea often begins even before the start of production. The process then continues through prototyping and the creation of a minimum viable product, into experimentation, and re-iteration based on real-world feedback. The success of a new product is rarely the result of an entrepreneur identifying an opportunity and then translating that opportunity into a working product. It's the result of their ability to adapt as customers begin using the product, to understand the market's reactions, and to make changes to suit customer behavior.

I saw that refinement first-hand during the development of Mdundo.

Refining the Idea of Mdundo

In 2012, Kresten's accelerator was struggling to find good deal flow. Too few valuable and scalable ideas were reaching the accelerator, and too few were making it through the assessment stage and meeting "Real-

Win-Worth-it" criteria. Accelerators select ideas but they depend on people bringing those ideas to them. In places like Silicon Valley, there's a constant flow of entrepreneurs with interesting concepts. Not all of them will meet the criteria for funding and development, but the stream is big enough for investors to be able to find and fund ideas that appear to have potential. In sub-Saharan Africa, with fewer serial entrepreneurs and a smaller number of people with the training and skill to develop those opportunities, the stream is narrower, shallower, and flows more slowly—though it is constantly strengthening!

So instead of waiting for ideas to come to the accelerator, Kresten and program manager Nikolai Barnwell decided to see if they could make something happen.

One of the benefits of spending time in Nairobi is that there's no shortage of great music. If you're prepared to head out to the local bars in the evening you can hear everything from cover bands and reggae to rhumba and traditional tribal music. The value of Africa's natural resources are well-known but the value of its cultural resources should really be much better known.

Kresten and Nikolai had had a chance to meet some of the city's musical artists as they explored Nairobi, and when they'd spoken to them after the performance, the artists had often complained about their lack of distribution options. Record labels in Africa are weak; they don't have the same kind of power over distribution and radio play that Universal and Warner do in the West. The local telecommunication firms were willing to offer music as a service with their phone packages but they demanded 80 percent of the sales revenue, leaving artists just 20 percent of the value of their music. And in a region with little disposable income and high data costs, the pull of pirated content was always strong, leaving the artists with too little leverage and too few earnings for their art.

That gap between the availability of a service and a market that wanted to consume it represented a business opportunity. Artists had valuable content but were struggling to bring it to customers and were getting a rough deal when they did. At the same time, although pirating is free, it's also inconvenient. Much of the music piracy in Africa at the time was carried out by people copying music from a friend's thumb drive onto their phones. If a business could give customers an easier way to consume music, they should be able to attract the attention of a large market, monetize that attention, and share the revenues with the artists. Musicians would get a better deal and the chance to deliver their music across the continent; music-lovers would get easier access to a product they wanted.

Kresten had an idea for an African digital music service. The idea appeared to meet a real need. If the service got its proposition, design, and marketing right, it looked like it should be able to hold its place even if it inspired competitors. And the popularity of music and the size of the potential market meant that should the service succeed, the effort would certainly be worthwhile. The idea met "Real-Win-Worth-it" criteria.

The question was whether it would work. Were there specific challenges in African markets that would prevent the idea of a digital music service from scaling in the region? What adjustments would the service need to make to the music streaming business model to work in an African context? Could the company find the talent it needed to build the product? Could it form and implement partnerships and agreements in an environment with weak courts? Would customers take up the offer? Would there be any interest at all in an African digital music service or was the market and the environment so different that the idea just wouldn't work?

There was only one way to find out.

88mph had an entrepreneur-in-residence. Martin Nielsen was a young, Danish business school student who was looking for a placement and had heard what 88mph was doing. He had cold-called Kresten from London and asked if he wanted any help. Kresten brought Martin out to Kenya and set him to work with the accelerator's clients, refining their business models and helping them to develop their companies.

Kresten prepared a one-pager for Martin that described the service he had in mind and gave him a budget of $25,000. He asked him to spend a few hours a week trying to see if he could build some sort of proof of concept.

Martin didn't know much about the music industry at the time—any more than Kresten did—and he knew even less about the music industry in sub-Saharan Africa, but he got to work. He would have a few months and a small budget to see if Mdundo—the kind of mobile music business that had long worked in Europe and the US—could take off in Kenya.

Martin quickly saw that the system couldn't work exactly like Spotify.

Data in Africa is expensive. South Africa's Vodacom offers data bundles by the hour and by the day, with special rates for night owls looking to save money at the cost of sleep. Customers looking to splash out can spend 229 rand for 3 gigabytes a month. That's a little over $12 in a country where the average annual salary is only about $1,200. In terms of purchasing power, that's like an average American paying almost $500 a month for their mobile data—and still barely getting enough to watch three movies.

Kenya is better but it's still not cheap. A 30-day, 3 gigabyte bundle from Airtel, with 50 megabytes of free Whatsapp costs 300 shillings, about $2.82. But little more than half of formally employed Kenyans earn more than 30,000 shillings (about $280) a month.[72]

So instead of subscribing to data, people in Africa tend to buy airtime in advance. They purchase scratch cards that let them recharge their phones with limited amounts of time and data. The telco industry in Africa has to use a unique business model that matches its consumers' ability to pay—and Mdundo would need to do the same. Trying to sell subscriptions to a mobile streaming service in the way that Spotify does would always have appealed to too thin a band of consumers capable of paying for it.

So the first incarnation of Mdundo wasn't a streaming service. It was a scratch card that customers could purchase and use to download songs. With an initial budget of just $25,000, Martin didn't have the funds to produce a large number of cards and test the market to see how well they sold. But he was able to persuade brands including Nokia, Heineken, and Airtel to sponsor the cards; they'd pay for their production in return for printing their names on the back.

---

[72] Babu Tendu, "Half of employed Kenyans earn less than Sh30,000 a month," ureport, November 25, 2019, https://www.standardmedia.co.ke/ureport/article/2001350746/half-of-employed-kenyans-earn-less-than-sh30-000-a-month

Without labels and their giant catalogues of rights, Martin also couldn't build an inventory of licensed music quickly as Spotify had been able to do. Instead, Martin signed up artists one by one, persuading them to make their music available to listeners on his digital platform. Mdundo soon had a stock of music it could offer, scratch cards it could sell, and once 88mph's CTO, Jura Sidorenko, had knocked up a simple music program to deliver the songs, it had a music service. Martin had a functioning business.

Over the next six months, it became clear that the idea wasn't working. To attract customers and give artists revenue, the company was giving the scratch cards to artists with the idea that they would sell them to their fans and earn revenues as their fans downloaded their songs. The plan was that when those music lovers reached the site, Mdundo would then be able to sell them more songs from other artists and share the sales revenue.

But instead of selling the cards, the artists were giving them away. Customers would come to the store and take their free songs but because they hadn't paid, they wouldn't purchase anything else. The cards, too, were difficult to produce. The manufacturers were used to dealing with much larger numbers than Mdundo was ordering. The scratch card system was generating interest and buzz, and attracting users, but it wasn't making money.

"It gave artists some merchandise in their hands so they were shouting out about it on social media," recalls Martin. "It gave us a lot of PR and press and excitement because it was something that was actually quite innovative." But financially, it didn't work.

Mdundo needed to find another way of delivering its product. The idea needed more refinement.

Eventually Martin did something that couldn't happen in the West: he agreed to give users free content with an option to download songs. To avoid cannibalizing the artists' sales, the download files are relatively low quality and they still include ads. But today Mdundo lets users keep songs without paying for them because the company knows that if customers don't download them on Mdundo, they won't stream them—and they will download pirated versions somewhere else. Fans now have a legitimate place to access music and Mdundo splits the advertising revenues with the artists. It now reaches many millions of people annually in Kenya and Tanzania alone, and is active across the continent with a total of +6 million unique users every month. The case of Mdundo illustrates the importance of building an offering that fits the demand from your customer segment. It sounds simple, but the reality is that many start-ups fail because they never find a product/market fit.

So idea generation in sub-Saharan Africa still depends on the same criteria and process as ideas everywhere else. Individuals are the best sources of new concepts. Groups are the best tools to begin the process of selecting and filtering those ideas. But as the idea heads out into the wild, businesses in Africa can expect to make some serious refinements—including the kinds of changes that they wouldn't expect to make in a different region.

That refinement stage isn't the only part of idea generation that has special significance in sub-Saharan Africa. The region also provides an opportunity to shorten the idea generation and selection phases by taking ideas that have already proven their value elsewhere. It was much easier to plan, then refine Mdundo knowing that Spotify had already created a successful model elsewhere.

One characteristic of building businesses in Africa is the temptation to develop ideas not through the generation of multiple concepts followed by discussion and culling, but through the replication of products and services that are already popular in Europe, the US, or in China. Entrepreneurs see a continent of more than a billion people which that service or product has yet to reach, and they try to build a version that Africans will use. Instead of trying to generate ideas to uniquely solve African problems, they attempt to replicate foreign ideas in Africa's markets.

It's a reasonable strategy, but one that throws up its own challenges.

Idea Replication in Africa

Idea replication isn't just an opportunity for Africa, of course. Much of China's tech environment is built on idea replication. Baidu is a Chinese version of Google, just as YouKu is a Chinese YouTube, and Didi DaChe is a local, Chinese Uber rival that ended up partnering with the company. Even in Western markets, idea replication is a valid way for entrepreneurs and investors to grow businesses and expand the reach of useful services.

In 2011, when AirBnB was four years old, the company ran into an unexpected problem. The founders, Brian Chesky, Joe Gebbia, and Nathan Blecharcyzk, had done the hardest work. They'd funded the company's early days by selling election-themed breakfast cereals. They'd spent three months in Y Combinator, a start-up accelerator, refining their business model. They'd found that people were willing to rent out their homes and that travelers were willing to stay in them. The company had just booked its millionth customer and was sitting on a pile of capital, ready to scale. That meant expanding into Europe, a market they knew they would have to conquer if they were serious about growth.

But as AirBnB started to draw up plans to grow from a one-office start-up based in San Francisco to an international travel company, Chesky noticed that his customers were starting to receive unsolicited emails from a European firm offering a similar service.

Wimdu was a travel site owned by the Samwer brothers, three German entrepreneurs who had become billionaires by replicating US companies in Europe before the American original got there first. Either they would try to conquer a market using a proven idea, or they would aim to establish a foothold, then sell the company to the original firm. In 1999, the Samwer brothers had sold Alando, an online auction site, to eBay for $54 million. The eBay clone was only a hundred days old. In 2007, Holtzbrinck Group, publishers of *Die Zeit* newspaper, paid 100 million Euros for StudiVZ, the brothers' German version of Facebook. In 2010, Groupon paid them 100 million Euros for MyCityDeal, a clone of its own service that threatened the company's ability to scale. As Reid Hoffman and Chris Yeh describe in *Blitzscaling: The Lightning Path to Building Massively Valuable Companies,* AirBnB took a different approach. Instead of buying Wimdu, Chesky and his team raised $112 million in venture capital, bought Accoleo, a smaller German AirBnB clone, and took Wimdu in its own back yard.[73]

---

[73] Reid Hoffman and Chris Yeh, *Blitzscaling: The Lightning Path to Building Massively Valuable Companies,* Currency, 2018

The Samwer Brothers might not have been too disappointed. By 2017, Zalando, their clone of Zappos, was worth more than $10 billion.

So idea replication can work anywhere but it doesn't always work everywhere. Despite frequent attempts by banks and fintech companies, digital payments still haven't taken off in all of Europe and the US in the same way that they have in Africa and China, where fewer people had access to credit and debit cards. Ankerbox was a US-based copy of a product popular in China that lets people rent battery packs for their mobile phones. Similar products can be found in even the smallest bars and eateries in China's towns; in the US, Ankerbox's battery banks lasted less than a year in a place where battery anxiety is a smaller issue.

Idea generation is more complex than waiting for an epiphany in the shower. Similarly, idea replication demands more than simply looking for an idea that works in one area and quickly copying it in another region before the idea's originator gets there first.

Professor Filipe Santos is the Dean and Chaired Professor at Católica-Lisbon School of Business and Economics in Portugal. He was a faculty member at INSEAD, and an expert on social entrepreneurship who teaches about venture replication. He divides idea replication into a framework made up of three parts.

Understanding the Business

The first part is the clarification of the core business concept. Before a business can replicate an idea, it first has to understand the business model and know how it creates value in a novel way. That means identifying everything that has to happen in order for the idea to create that value, the dependencies between those activities, and any additional activities that add more value. The company also needs to make sure that the idea doesn't depend on any proprietary elements or assets. Any local entrepreneur can replicate AirBnB by matching travelers with spare living space in a city; they'll need to come up with their own search algorithm if they're building a local version of Google.

Like idea generation as a whole, the idea also has to be worth it—and be worthwhile in the different contexts of its new region. AirBnB started in San Francisco when the founders rented rooms in their apartment to designers visiting a conference at a time when hotels were fully booked.

San Francisco's accommodation shortage has given it some of the most expensive real estate in the world, so the idea had value for both visitors and for hard-pressed renters. The idea would have less value in a city or a region with a large accommodation supply, low rent, and little traveler demand. As we've seen, there's little point in rolling out an African Netflix if the number of people with access to fast, reliable data connections can't justify the expense. The desire for the service might exist, but until the infrastructure was in place to connect customers to the service, the effort wasn't worthwhile.

Context Factors

The second part of Santos's strategy focuses on context, which he divides between "context necessary factors" and "context success factors." The former refers to all of the factors and conditions that the context needs in order for the idea to function. A mobile money network—like a bank of rentable mobile batteries—can't work without the common use of mobile devices.

Context success factors are less concrete and include the cultural, technical, and demographic factors that a business implementing the idea would need in order to be successful. Ecommerce requires Internet connections and electronic devices that enable people to make purchases, but it also needs delivery systems, consumer trust, and a payment infrastructure that can accept and transfer funds.

Those success factors are themselves defined by their context. Visa has issued more than 14 million cards in Kenya, and Mastercard is active in 48 African countries so a desk-study would probably conclude that the payment infrastructure for ecommerce is in place. In theory, customers in sub-Saharan Africa should be able to place orders online using their credit cards just like a customer in the US or Europe. But anyone who spends a bit of time in Kenya would know that credit cards are used very rarely to make payments. According to Visa, banks have marketed the cards as ATM cards for withdrawing cash. Few customers are even aware that they can also use the card to make payments. Consumers need to trust ecommerce infrastructure but they also need to know how it works and the options available.

The Replication Format

Finally, the third part of Santos's strategy concerns how the idea is replicated. Entrepreneurs can license part or all of the idea from its originator, benefitting from its brand identity and giving their own business access to any necessary proprietary assets. They can also form joint ventures, an arrangement that demands close co-ordination between both partners. Or they can re-invent the idea, which means that it has no brand benefits, access to proprietary assets, or help with implementation. The company will be competing with the idea originator if that company ever decides to enter the market but they'll also be working with an idea that's been proven in one region and will be free to adapt and refine it to match the new region.

The replication strategy will often be a compromise between the rating of the suitability of different parameters: the fit of the business model to the context; the complexity of the business process; the value of the brand in the new market; and the strength of any proprietary code or designs. The rating of each of those parameters determines whether the strategy leans towards reinvention, licensing, or a joint venture. If there is a high fit on all parameters you probably want to work towards a license-agreement or joint venture, whereas a low fit will motivate you to re-invent.

For instance, BeautyClick was a replication of Mayvenn.com—a US venture backed by Andreessen Horowitz, Cross Culture Ventures, and Trinity Ventures, as well as a number of famous athletes and musicians including Serena Williams, Andre Iguodala, and Jimmy Lovine. When we assessed the optimal replication strategy, we ended up with the following:

The overall concept of the business model and the website made replication attractive. We could certainly build an ecommerce site focused on hair weaves. But the African ecommerce market has issues in regards to payments, delivery, and trust so the fit of the full business model and workflow on the site was low. The complexity of the supply chain also suggested a potential benefit in leveraging the supply chain and quality assurance that Mayvenn had already created. But what finally made us reject the idea of a licensing agreement with Mayvenn was the fact that consumers in sub-Saharan Africa have little brand loyalty when it comes to weaves and wigs so the value of the Mayvenn brand in Africa would be extremely low.

Rating	Business model fit	Complexity of business process	Brand value in a new market	Strength of proprietary code/designs
Low	Re-invent		Re-invent	
Middle		License		License
High				

Table 3. Replication assessment of Mayvenn.com

Again, the refinement is important. An established idea placed in a new context might require both necessary and success factors but other factors that are present can also change the idea itself.

Replicating Shopify in Africa

The development of Sky.Garden applied a replication strategy to Shopify, a Canadian business that provides online storefronts for more than a million merchants in over 175 countries.

Shopify started when founder Tobi Lütke wanted to build an online snowboard store and discovered that the software he had created was more valuable than the products his store was selling. His idea solved a problem for other business owners who wanted to sell online but who lacked the skills to build their own ecommerce site.

Sellers in sub-Saharan Africa suffer from the same problem. Many would benefit from the extra reach that an online store would bring them but few know how to build their own websites. Their need matches Shopify's core business concept.

The idea also needs a context in which people are able to place online orders. Although digital penetration in Kenya isn't as deep as it is in Canada, devices are less sophisticated, and the Internet connections slower and more expensive, there are enough people with smartphones and an understanding of online shopping to give a Shopify for Africa the necessary success factors.

Building Successful Businesses in Sub-Saharan Africa

But to be successful, a business that replicated Shopify in sub-Saharan Africa would need to solve another problem that doesn't exist in places like Ottawa: the specific challenge of bringing goods from the store to the customer. Even Amazon still relies on the US Postal Service to deliver its orders, but a business in Nairobi would not want to depend on the efficiency of the local postal service for order fulfillment. You need to solve last-mile distribution in a different way and, as an ecommerce player, take a much stronger lead in this part of the value chain.

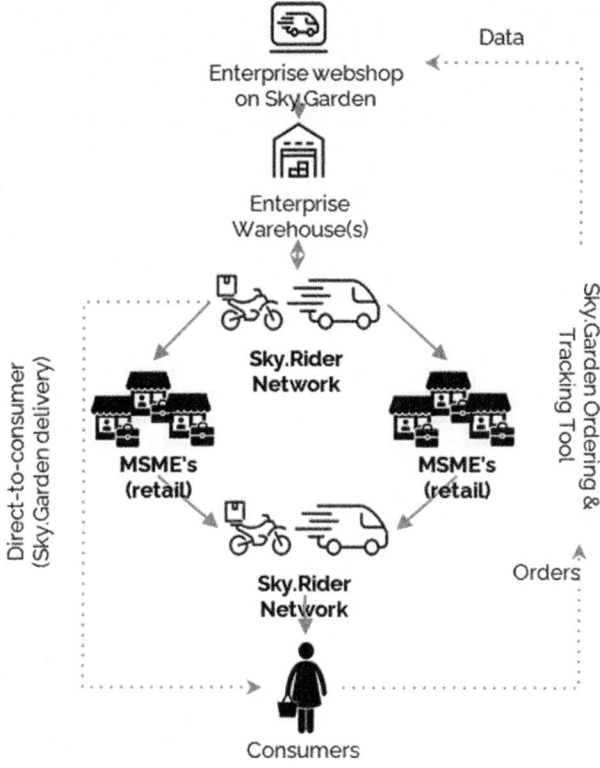

Figure 8. Sky.Garden direct-to-consumer delivery model (Source: Sky.Garden pitch-deck)

So even though the idea itself could be replicated relatively easily and without the need to license proprietary technology, Sky.Garden needed to refine the idea in order to make it successful in a sub-Saharan African context. The company partnered with delivery service firms who pick up the goods from bricks and mortar stores and deliver them to customers' doors. As I pointed out, most payments are made with mobile money, but actually that is the least of the challenges for ecommerce players. Because of a lack of trust, payments tend to be made on delivery and not, as we are used to in Europe and US, when ordering. This, of course, gives extra distribution challenges. Fast delivery is key to avoid unsuccessful deliveries and higher costs.

So replication can work. The gap between the proving of an idea in one market and its expansion into a new market is an opportunity for local entrepreneurs who keep an eye on what's happening around the world. If they can gain a clear understanding of the core business concept, see that the new context has the factors necessary for the idea's success, and select an appropriate method of replication, an entrepreneur can implement a successful business idea in their own region before the creator of that idea has a chance to expand. Local customers won't have to wait to enjoy the service, and even if the originator of the idea does reach that region, customers might benefit from the competition. When Uber tried to compete in China with Didi Chuxing, its China-based clone, both companies poured money into market acquisition. Uber is reported to have spent $2 billion to lower fees and subsidize rides. Didi spent even more to win in its own territory, rolling out half a dozen new products, including carpooling, car rental, and inter-city buses.[74] Didi won. Uber pulled out of the market in return for an 18 percent share in Didi but the winners overall were China's travelers. Owning a car in a Chinese city is expensive and often difficult; Didi's idea replication improved the country's travel infrastructure and made life in cities easier

Similarly, Mdundo found that it couldn't offer music streaming but it could still deliver music online to mobile phones based on an ad-supported freemium model. Sky.Garden needed to add a delivery service and mobile money features to its offer to make it attractive enough in a Kenyan context, but it's still an ecommerce platform that gives business owners an easy way to sell online.

---

[74] James Crabtree, "Didi Chuxing took on Uber and won. Now it's taking on the world," Wired, February 9, 2018 https://www.wired.co.uk/article/didi-chuxing-china-startups-uber

But Sky.Garden has made another refinement. Shopify uses a Software as a Service (SaaS) model that charges a set of monthly fees (plus a small payment transaction fee) regardless of the volume of the client's sales. Ecommerce adoption in sub-Saharan Africa is significantly lower than in the West and is not the first stop for either businesses or buyers looking to buy and sell goods. As a result, entrepreneurs in Africa are less likely to risk committing to a monthly fee unless they know that they're going to make that money back. In a context that has less experience of—and less trust in—ecommerce, Sky.Garden needs to lower the risk for store-owners and make it easier for them to come on board. It does that by changing the business model. Instead of simply charging a subscription fee, the company adds an 8 percent service fee to every transaction.

"We decided to remove any barriers of adoption by having a free-to-join platform that would not impact the seller in any way by way of cost," explains Daniel Maison, Sky.Garden's CEO. "Having a transparent and simple commercial model makes it easy to onboard new sellers organically, maintain retention and prove value without the need of merchants having to pay to do so. This model works for this market."

In time, once sellers have become used to selling online and they've built a customer base, they can switch to an SaaS model that offers lower commissions and better marketing tools.

That refinement doesn't just make the proposition more attractive for cautious clients who can get up and running without any money down. It also gives Sky.Garden a stake in every business and a reason to work with them for their success. The more a seller on Sky.Garden succeeds, the more Sky.Garden will earn. The company is incentivized to teach sellers how to market themselves, deliver good customer service, and offer products that their customers want to buy.

That small change to the business model, caused by the context in which the idea is being constructed, has a big impact and strengthens ecommerce in the region.

Sky.Garden's billboards made it to Brilliant Ads

Developing Business Models in Africa

Both idea development and idea replication require refinement and adaptation. Whether the idea is new or a copy of a business model already working in a different part of the world it will need to fit the region's context and the characteristics of its customer base. Phil Parker, INSEAD's Chair Professorship of Management Science, has pointed out that business models tend to scale within the same market segment. The people at the top of the pyramid buy the same branded handbags, stay in the same hotel suites, and fly in the same private jets whether they're from Dubai, Durban, or Dallas. But for people at the bottom of the pyramid, life can differ dramatically around the world. In the United States, among those earning less than $30,000 a year, more than half have home broadband.[75] They're also likely to live in a household with a car and a widescreen television. They'll certainly have a refrigerator. Using a digital service like Spotify—or Mdundo—requires a smartphone and access to Internet service. Those requirements are easily met even among low-income consumers in Europe and the US. They're met less often in Africa, where the same service is aiming at a smaller slice of the population, and one higher up the pyramid. Being poor in America isn't the same as being poor in Africa, so services aimed at the bottom and middle of the pyramid have to adapt to the region.

"The business model in one area will not work in another area necessarily," explains Phil Parker. "If you don't have the same segmentation structure in two countries it's not likely to work."

When a business takes an idea that works in one region and attempts to replicate it in another region that has a different segmentation structure, different purchasing power, and different degrees of consumer trust, it needs to make changes.

One aspect of the business idea that can change is the business model itself.

---

[75] Monica Anderson and Madhumitha Kumar, "Digital divide persists even as lower-income Americans make gains in tech adoption," Pew Research Center, May 7, 2019

https://www.pewresearch.org/fact-tank/2019/05/07/digital-divide-persists-even-as-lower-income-americans-make-gains-in-tech-adoption/

We've already seen this happening to some extent. Mdundo needed to adapt its business model to take into account the relatively high cost of data. Instead of giving away a low quality streaming service and charging for additional functions and the removal of interruptions as Spotify does, it had to allow downloads and earn from advertising. Because Sky.Garden operates in a region whose market has unreliable revenue streams and high concern about committing to a monthly fee, it needed to find an alternative business model to supplement SaaS.

It is possible to implement an idea in a region that appears unsuitable and make it work, but you might have to change the idea's business model entirely. The "Business Model Canvas" is a common template for documenting existing business models and for developing new ones. It contains a number of elements:

Customer segments

These are the business's customers, the market groups that an enterprise can try to reach and serve. While the segments may remain the same across regions and contexts, the populations in those segments may change. Both Spotify and Mdundo would include in their customer segments anyone who enjoys listening to music, and both would expect low earners to use an ad-supported business model. But Spotify can expect many of those free users to upgrade into paid subscribers as their income grows. At the end of March 2020, Spotify reported having 286 million monthly active users, 130 million of whom were subscribers, a ratio of almost one paying customer for every two free users. In 2019, the company earned 1.6 billion euros from paid subscribers and 217 million euros in ad-supported revenue. It has two customer segments: low-earners, such as students who listen for free; and higher income earners who pay to hear what they want. The company is able to offer a different revenue model for each.

For Mdundo, the customer segment that includes low-earners will be much larger, and the ratio of paying customers to free customers much smaller. That means that the revenue model for non-paying market segments has to be robust; the small size of the market segment that can afford to pay for a subscription doesn't allow it to subsidize free listeners until they're ready to convert. The different balance between the customer segments requires a different revenue model. The solution isn't only used by Mdundo. It's also used by other successful music services in Asia such as India's JioSaavn which has 100 million users.

It's also worth noting that Spotify lost 77 million euros in the last quarter of 2019 and expects losses of between 150 million and 250 million euros in 2020.[76] The company was founded in 2006. A company implementing a similar idea in sub-Saharan Africa would have much less time to create functioning revenue models.

It's important to remember too that customer segments can vary within sub-Saharan Africa. At BeautyClick we expanded into South Africa in 2017 and opened an office in Johannesburg, replicating the business model from Kenya. The move should have been straightforward. The market in South Africa is more ecommerce-mature and Kenya had already worked as a test market. But in practice we were missing one important partnership in Johannesburg: a courier service that was willing to take cash on delivery. For safety reasons, the couriers would not allow their employees to drive around with cash. In Kenya, payment on delivery is performed with mobile money, a standard in the ecommerce market. In South Africa, we thought pre-payments with credit cards was much more common. I had even spoken about it with two of 88mph's portfolio companies that had specialized in ecommerce in the country.

Our problem was that the target segment for BeautyClick was colored women aged 24–45, sometimes living in dangerous areas. Among that segment, credit card payments were not common. In addition, the major ecommerce player in South Africa—Takealot.com (the Amazon of South Africa) and its subsidiaries—had employed its own delivery service, which did accept cash on delivery. The market now expected cash on delivery as an option but it was very hard to offer unless you were a part of Takealot.com, something that consumers found very hard to understand. We decide to pull out of the market for a while.

So why did I not get a red flag when talking to the 88mph portfolio companies? I was naïve. I failed to dig into the details and understand that their target segment is upper class people living in expensive parts of Johannesburg who are frequent users of credit cards.

---

[76] Spotify Technology, *Letter to Shareholders,* April 29, 2020 https://s22.q4cdn.com/540910603/files/doc_financials/2020/q1/Shareholder-Letter-Q1-2020-[Final]-(1).pdf

Value propositions

Value propositions are the products and services that deliver value to a customer segment. The products and services that a business idea delivers may be the same in different regions but the value that customer segments place on those products and services will vary, and that variety will affect the nature of the business model too.

The relative value that music listeners will place on the ability to listen to music, for example, is likely to be similar in New York and Nairobi. But the value that a market segment places on the ease of being able to listen to that music without accessing illegal download sites will change with location. Music-lovers in sub-Saharan Africa may feel less concern about illegally downloading music they can't afford to buy than customers in Europe who have the ability to pay artists for their work. That difference in value increases the importance of a freemium business model in Africa that can compete with pirate sites.

Similarly, small business owners in regions with a developed ecommerce landscape place a higher value on the ownership of an online store. Because that value is less clear in sub-Saharan African countries, a company implementing that business idea needs to lower the cost of entry and increase the apparent value of the offer by including delivery services.

Key partners

Every business needs suppliers and partners to function. Partners can include complementary businesses, mentors, advisors, grant providers, etc. Most important, though, is to map out the value chain and identify key partners with the motivation of optimization and economic results, reduction of risk, and acquisition of particular resources, such as tapping into an already existing client base, etc.

We've already seen how the absence of partners who can provide funding will affect business models in Africa. The difficulty of finding the funds needed to scale means that business models implemented in the region need to be able to generate profits much more quickly than they do in a different area. A Ugandan entrepreneur presenting a business idea can't talk about a model that relies on customer acquisition in the short and medium term in order to generate profits in the long term. The funding is unlikely to last long enough to generate those profits.

Partnerships are also often underpinned by legal agreements. As we'll see in the next chapter, the weakness of courts across sub-Saharan Africa means that contracts are less valuable in enforcing co-operation between partners than the continued delivery of benefits for all parties.

Key activities

The most important actions that a business must take for its model to be successful have to align with the model's value propositions. Those activities are likely to be similar across regions. Like Spotify, Mdundo needed to build a database to store and retrieve songs. Sky.Garden employs coders and designers to create templates. Digital businesses everywhere need data analysts to crunch the numbers, target marketing efforts, and review activity. But regional differences can also force entrepreneurs to take actions that they wouldn't take anywhere else.

The absence of record labels with a catalogue of rights in Kenya, for example, meant that while Spotify was able to sign license agreements with the major record labels in the world, Martin Nielsen had to spend a great deal of time signing up artists one-by-one. Mdundo eventually had to build a self-service up-load business for artists. It would have been much easier and quicker to have been able to call up a record company and negotiate access to the company's entire library. But that signing activity also allowed Martin to build close and trusted relationships with artists, to understand their challenges directly, and to craft services and offers that benefitted them. Mdundo now manages more than 80,000 artists directly. In the absence of enforceable partnership contracts, that understanding and the reliable delivery of benefits to artists has given Mdundo valuable relationships and helped ensure its success.

Mdundo logo flashing at Times Square

Key resources

Key resources are one of the most important assets the business needs for its model to be successful. In sub-Saharan Africa, those resources have tended to be the ore in the ground and the machines that dig them out. For companies building digital solutions, they might include proprietary IP but more importantly, they tend to consist of staff. Countries like Singapore and Israel have been able to build successful hi-tech industries in the absence of natural resources because they have invested heavily in education and talent-spotting. China, too, strongly emphasizes education with its annual *gaokao* college entrance exams, a stressful rite of passage for both parents and school-leavers. It's made easier by private tuition. More than nine out of ten Chinese parents are believed to have paid for private tuition for their children to help them improve their exam results.[77]

---

[77] HSBC. *The value of education: Higher and higher. Global report.* London: HSBC Holdings plc., 2017 https://link.springer.com/article/10.1007%2Fs10902-020-00258-0

As we'll see in the next chapter, acquiring key human resources in sub-Saharan Africa presents its own unique challenges.

Customer relationships

The kind of relationship the company can create with a customer segment can also be affected by context. Digital companies are often able to build direct relationships with customers, using data to build segmented lists that create unique relationships based on customer activity. Customers who always respond to email newsletters or who share the most social media content can receive rewards and bonuses that encourage them to continue sharing and make more purchases.

Brands in the West can use those relationships to build loyalty but in sub-Saharan Africa, that loyalty is thinner, and the pull of competitors can be much stronger. Again and again people underestimate the price-elasticity for many product categories across sub-Saharan Africa.

At BeautyClick, we gave hairdressers an online store and invited them to encourage their clients to review styles of hairpieces, and place their orders. That model, which had worked in the US, didn't work in Kenya. The hairdressers weren't used to ordering online and they didn't understand the workflow. Instead of simply placing orders that BeautyClick could deliver for the hairdressers to apply, the hairdressers would call the company every time they wanted to make a purchase for their clients.

So BeautyClick changed the model and adjusted the nature of the relationship. The company gave the hairdressers marketing material so that they could sell the products to their clients themselves. BeautyClick's relationship with hairdressers changed from business enabler to a kind of marketing coach focused on a particular product. That model worked until hairdressers realized that they could sell hairpieces to their clients, and they started looking for cheaper, rival products that gave them bigger profits. Nairobi has a shopping street called River Road where it's possible to buy anything, including hairpieces that have managed to avoid the 40 percent import taxes that are applicable in Kenya.

Digital Africa

Part of the BeautyClick team presenting values

Much of a company's relationship with customers is built on brand trust, a sentiment that has different strengths in different regions.

Channels

Customer relationships describe the interaction that a business model creates between a company and its customer segments. The channels are the tools that the business uses to reach those customer segments.

Different business models can use a range of different channels to engage audiences, from print and billboard advertising to direct sales and television advertising. For technology companies, one channel that's particularly popular is content. Companies like Refinery20 and PopSugar have used content to build a following that they can then convert into customers by promoting specific products.

Sabrina Dorman, a former Jumia executive, attempted to use a similar business model in Kenya when she set up Zumi. Dorman's experience at Jumia had shown her that launching an ecommerce business would require more capital to sustain than her funding would allow so she used a content-based business model to attract the attention of the female, fashion-conscious customer segment she wanted to reach.

Building a website, hiring writers, and attracting an audience all happened quickly. Within just a few months of launch, Zumi had around a quarter of a million users. The company raised more funds and expanded into Nigeria, quickly reaching an audience of around a million followers.

With the content channel reaching the desired market segment, Zumi then started selling directly to customers—and that was when it became clear that while it's possible to use content channels to reach audiences in sub-Saharan Africa, converting that audience is much harder. People are happy to consume free content online but they're still reluctant to buy products. Last mile delivery added to costs, and in the absence of brand trust, buyers worried that they wouldn't like the product once they could actually see it and touch it.

So Zumi capitalized on a different kind of trust. It encouraged audiences to act as a network of sales agents, recommending products that owners of small businesses could buy. Soon, the company found that the product that sold the most was secondhand clothing, which the company sold wholesale to retailers. Dorman closed down the content channel and focused on a B2B apparel business.

Cost structure

The costs the company incurs to operate its business model are a concern in every business model—and every business model attempts to reduce them as much as possible. For tech companies, the biggest expenses tend to be the engineers required to build the technology and the costs of customer acquisition, but with the very important characteristic that the marginal cost of serving one additional client becomes very low. This is an extremely strong factor in many businesses across Africa, where the willingness (and ability) to pay is also very low. Many business models fail simply because the marginal revenue never becomes higher than the marginal cost even at scale. When that happens not even a billion customers will help you build a profitable business.

In addition digital companies in sub-Saharan Africa face two particular challenges in the cost structures of their business models: the pressure to minimize costs when funding is scarce; and the cost of retaining customers they have already paid to acquire in a context with minimal brand loyalty and high price-sensitivity.

Both of those are challenges but this is also one area where digital companies in sub-Saharan Africa have an advantage. Although we'll see that finding skilled engineers isn't easy or straightforward, talent can cost much less in the region than it does outside it, helping to reduce one of the biggest costs that digital companies face.

Revenue stream

Finally, the revenue stream is the cash the company generates from each customer segment it serves. Those revenue streams might take the form of subscription payments, direct sales, commissions, or ad views, for example. It sounds very simple but most entrepreneurs in Africa, Europe, the US or Asia understand how hard it is to create sustainable and stable revenue streams. In sub-Saharan Africa, however, businesses have to face an additional issue. Because the use of credit cards is very limited, most payments happen via mobile money or cash. But most mobile money systems lack the option of subscription payments so the user has to actively pay the subscription every day, week, month, or year, raising churn rate to a very high level.

At BeautyClick, the team once asked the board if they could let clients pay in installments. There was a huge demand for the service but it was an idea that, because of the risks of default, we had previously rejected. When we discussed the team's proposal in detail though, I realized that they were not suggesting a credit offer. Clients simply wanted a solution that would help them save to buy the product. For example, they might pay in four installments and only receive the product once the last installment was paid. Cash remained king. From a cashflow perspective, the solution was, of course, very appealing. So why are product credit companies not flooding the market with savings and installment solutions? Some product financing companies have entered the continent over the last couple of years, but many of them are still struggling despite very high interest rates. The issue is simply data! It is very hard to find valid credit history for individuals and even if you can find it, the risk of default is still large. The sector continues to develop day by day.

Each of those parts of a business model is adjustable. By changing the cost structure or testing a new marketing channel entrepreneurs can turn business ideas into new ventures that deliver value to customer segments in new ways. That adjustment happens all the time.

Entrepreneurs turning ideas into businesses in sub-Saharan Africa will need to be aware of all these parts of the business model canvas and be prepared to refine them to fit the context. They need to generate business ideas, select them and adjust them, and they need to understand the difference between the way a business idea works in one region and how it might work in Africa.

They also have to be able to recruit, train, and hold on to staff, and build partnerships. That's what we'll look at in the next chapter.

Chapter Six

Recruiting People and Building Partnerships in African Start-Ups

Imagine that you are a new graduate in Denmark. You will have just completed five years of study. You will have a qualification equivalent to a master's degree. You will have enjoyed a good education and you will likely have some on-the-job experience. You will have no significant student loans and no obligations to anyone.

That's partly because throughout your studies, neither you nor your parents will have needed to pay tuition fees. From the age of eighteen, if you were no longer living at home, the government will even have given you a grant now worth DKK 6,244 ($989) a month to help you pay rent and buy food.

By the time you have completed your studies, your path ahead will be clear and there will be nothing holding you back.

Few countries have education systems as generous as Denmark's. In the US, graduates leave university with an average $32,731 of student debt.[78] In the UK, the figure is around £36,000 ($47,111).[79]

---

[78] Bennett G. Boggs, "U.S. Student Loans and Debt Levels Set Record: What's a Legislature to Do?" *A Legislator's Toolkit for the New World of Higher Education, National Conference of State Legislatures,* May 2019 https://www.ncsl.org/Portals/1/Documents/educ/Student-Loans-And-Debt_v02.pdf

[79] Paul Bolton, "Student loan statistics," House of Commons Library, December 16, 2019 https://commonslibrary.parliament.uk/research-briefings/sn01079/

But British graduates don't have to begin repaying their loans until their income reaches £26,575 ($34,777) a year. Only about 30 percent of them will pay their debt back in full, and as they start work, few will have any other obligations tying them down. Graduates in the US and UK might need to pay their own rent and buy their own food once they take their first jobs, but they won't have to contribute to their own families. In fact, it's more likely that they'll know that if their first placements don't pay a high enough salary or don't work out, they can always return home and benefit from the support of their family until they're able to get back on their feet. At worst, the (welfare) state will help them until they can help themselves.

None of that is true in sub-Saharan Africa.

If you were a new graduate in Nairobi, there is a good chance that you would be leaving college with heavy debts. Students in Kenya are expected to pay their own tuition fees, around Sh50,000 ($461) per year. The Higher Education Loans Board, or Helb, is able to lend students a maximum of Sh60,000, little more than enough to cover a single year of tuition, and can provide bursaries of no more than Sh8,000, an amount that doesn't even cover a fraction of the course's total fees.[80]

The loans carry an interest rate of 4 percent a year and repayments are supposed to begin within a year of graduation even though only around 45 percent of graduates will be in full-time employment six months to a year after graduation.[81] In January 2020, Helb declared that it was pursuing 78,328 loan defaulters who had not responded to frequent threats of prosecution, credit bureau listings, and the deployment of

---

[80] Constant Munda, "Rich students gobble varsity bursaries and loans in Kenya," *Business Daily*, September 10, 2019
https://www.businessdailyafrica.com/datahub/Rich-students-gobble-varsity-bursaries-and-loans-in-Kenya/3815418-5267102-ujjo2nz/index.html

[81] Tristan McCowan, Moses Oketch, Ibrahim Oanda, "Towards a National Graduate Destinations Survey in Kenya: An Exploratory Study of Three Universities," *Higher Education Policy*, March 2017
https://www.researchgate.net/publication/315533148_Towards_a_National_Graduate_Destinations_Survey_in_Kenya_An_Exploratory_Study_of_Three_Universities

Recruiting People and Building Partnerships in African Start-Ups

debt recovery agents.[82] Because Helb is self-funding, the outstanding loans mean that 113,953 eligible students would not be able to receive loans in the current academic year, Helb declared.

But it's not just the loans—and the need to repay them shortly after graduation—that weighs on graduates in sub-Saharan Africa. They will also have obligations to their families. They may be the only sibling the family has been able to send to college, and having obtained a valuable education, they'll be expected to help: by sending money home; by paying for a sibling's school fees; by putting up relatives arriving in the city from the countryside; by paying for a parent's medical expenses.

Unlike a graduate in Denmark or the US or the UK, an African graduate starts their career laden with debts and obligations that have to be met immediately. Those obligations limit opportunities and affect plans. An entrepreneurial graduate who wants to start their own business or join a start-up can't pay their brother's school fees with warrants that vest in three years. They can't tell relatives that they'll share the profits when their company exits in a market that has seen few exits. Even as employees, graduates with good jobs have obligations that mean they often have a side-hustle and are always looking for the next opportunity.

I've seen the effect of those obligations a number of times in my own companies.

Shortly before one scheduled trip to Kenya, I received a call from the chief executive of one of my companies. For his protection, let's call him Sam.

"I'll come and pick you up at the airport," Sam told me. "There's something I want to discuss with you."

That wasn't what I wanted to hear. As welcoming as it is to be met at Jomo Kenyatta airport instead of having to line up for an Uber outside the terminal, a senior employee telling you that they need to talk is rarely good news. And while it's nice to be able to climb into the employee's brand new Mercedes 300 after a long flight, it's worrying when you remember that you're paying that employee $1,600 a month.

---

[82] Lynet Igadwah, "113,000 to miss student loans, Helb now warns," *Business Daily*, January 8, 2020 https://www.businessdailyafrica.com/economy/113-000-to-miss-student-loans/3946234-5411576-dj0903z/index.html

"I'm sorry," Sam said as we pulled away from the airport. "But I would like to quit."

"Really?" I asked, admiring the Mercedes' leather interior. "What happened? Is something wrong? Is there something I can do?"

"No, no. Everything is fine. But I've decided I would rather do something else. I'm going to import hard timber. From Congo."

"Cool," I said. "Hard timber. From Congo. Fair enough. If your mind is made up then I wish you luck. I hope it works out for you. So I'll try to find your replacement over the next couple of weeks. You'll be able to hand over to them before your termination period ends."

"Actually, that's what I wanted to talk to you about," said Sam. "I have a big shipment coming in next week, and I need to be at the border. So I'm leaving next week. Sorry about that."

Of course, Sam wasn't going to import hard timber from Congo. He was already importing hard timber from Congo, and he had been for a while. I also discovered that he owned two gas stations up country and was managing them at the same time that he was importing his timber—and while he was supposed to be working full-time in our company.

It's something that has happened to me more than once putting together a team in sub-Saharan Africa. You'll work hard to find people with the ability to do the job, assess them, and train them. You'll pay them a salary that matches their qualifications and their level of responsibility, typically about 30–40 percent more than they earned in their previous job—and you'll often feel that you've got a bargain. You'll have found someone with the same skill, drive, and ability of any high quality recruit anywhere in the world but the lower cost of living means that you'll be paying them a fraction of the salary you'd have to pay somewhere else. The starting salary for a computer programmer in the United States ranges from $50,000 to over $100,000, and if you're building a company in Silicon Valley, you can expect to pay even more.[83] In Nairobi, we pay around six million shillings ($58,000) a year for a top-end, experienced coder—about the same price a company in the US would pay for a new graduate.

---

[83] "Average Software Developer Salary," Payscale, last accessed September 15, 2020 https://www.payscale.com/research/US/Job=Software_Developer/Salary

But with that opportunity to recruit skilled talent for low cost and a minimal drain on seed funds come additional, unique challenges. You'll assume that your new recruit will dedicate themselves to the success of the business, but you might find that in order to pay their loans and meet their obligations, they also run a side hustle from your office. You'll expect them to be as driven and self-motivated as a start-up employee, and many will be. But you may also find that an education system that prioritizes obedience and rote-learning can beat out initiative and lower risk-taking. And you'll find too that while the region does have valuable talent, it also suffers from skills gaps which makes finding that talent particularly difficult.

Recruitment is one of the most crucial moments in the life of a company, and it should be done carefully. Businesses need to identify the key activities that they will need to undertake, the skills they will need to perform those activities, and the roles that employees will take in the company. And they have to know where to look to find the people to fill those roles—and how to attract them.

Building Effective Teams, Executing Well, and Creating Incentives in African Start-Ups

Finding good people is a challenge everywhere, especially in the technology industry. At the start of 2020, human resources firm ManpowerGroup reported that 54 percent of companies were suffering from skills shortages[84] while a 2019 survey from PwC found that 79 percent of global CEOs were concerned about the availability of key skills.[85] A year later, the survey found that only 18 percent of those chief executives thought that their company had made "significant progress" in creating an upskilling program.

---

[84] "Global Talent Shortages Hit Record Highs: ManpowerGroup Reveals How to Close the Skills Gap with New Research on What Workers Want," ManpowerGroup, January 17, 2020

https://www.manpowergroup.com/media-center/news-releases/global-talent-shortages-hit-record-high

[85] *23rd Annual Global CEO Survey: Navigating the rising tide of uncertainty,* PwC, 2020 https://www.pwc.com/gx/en/ceo-survey/2020/reports/pwc-23rd-global-ceo-survey.pdf

The challenge starts almost from the moment the company is formed. The first five hires that a company makes are critical, says Henning Piezunka, an Assistant Professor of Entrepreneurship and Family Enterprise at INSEAD. They help to define the ability of a company to continue to recruit. The best new hires are able to tell a company which other roles the firm needs, and which roles they might not have considered. They also attract other top talent. The best team members want to work with other people at the top of their game and will be reluctant to join firms that have only managed to gather people with no experience or reputation. Good first employees and known co-founders make the following rounds of recruitment easier.

But those initial recruits also have to bond. They have to be skilled and talented enough to deliver value and attract other hires, but also flexible enough to work together. Failure is likely to occur when teams are not strategically aligned in their goals. Company founders can vary in their degree of commitment or disagree about the desired rate of growth or the direction of the company. Even a team of highly-skilled individuals can continue to have significant skills gaps. Each of those factors can hold back the development of the company so it's vital for the founders to develop a recruitment plan. They need to know what skills they're going to need and how they're going to obtain them.

Recruitment planning, says Piezunka, should begin with a blank slate, without considering team members who are already on board, and as though you were an investor who needs to staff a team to execute an idea. The process then passes through five stages.

First, businesses need to identify the activities they plan to undertake. They need to list all the skills required for those activities, then group them into roles that possess those skills.

At Sky.Garden, for example, it was clear that we would need someone who could develop and maintain a large ecommerce site and its services. They'd need to have a particular set of coding skills, understand payment and order systems, and be up-to-date with design themes in order to create templates. We'd also need sales people with good communication skills who could work with merchants and guide them through the use of the service. At Mdundo, Martin Nielsen found that he needed journalists who could create content that would help to drive traffic to the site and generate interest in the artists he was signing.

Start-ups often discuss the benefits of outsourcing different services, but in a lot of ventures across Africa that discussion includes outsourcing tech development to places such as India or Eastern Europe. Jumia, for example, has most of its development operations in Portugal. Often, the argument for using local resources is knowledge of the context whereas the argument for using non-local resources is access to a larger and more experienced talent pool. I don't think there is a right or wrong approach, but if a venture decides to hire a non-local tech-team it is very important to have a product manager who understands the local market very well.

Businesses need to identify their activities in order to know the roles they need to fill.

The next step is to filter out activities that aren't core to the business. If recruitment is a challenge, only recruiting those people the company needs the most will make that challenge as small and manageable as possible. So the third stage of recruitment planning is to understand what the business can safely outsource, and where it will outsource from. Some of the services it buys may be essential but if they're not part of what makes the company unique, they don't need to be performed in-house.

About a million tech companies, for example, choose to outsource their server management to Amazon, including companies as large as Adobe, Slack, and Netflix. That server management is essential; without reliable servers, those global corporations can't function at all. But the servers aren't what make those companies unique, any more than running water is a special feature of a stay at a Hilton hotel. Even essential roles can be outsourced if they don't affect the company's unique proposition and they can be supplied by someone else more efficiently.

So although Sky.Garden depends on delivery drivers to pick up goods from merchants and deliver them to customers, none of those drivers are employees of the company. Sky.Garden is a technology company, not a delivery company. It can provide the delivery solution that both merchants and buyers need more cheaply and efficiently by working with outside suppliers—and without the need to recruit drivers, check their driving records, and track their performance.

Having identified the activities that the company needs to perform, created the roles that will perform those activities, and found outsourcing solutions for those activities that aren't key to the company's unique sales point, the fourth step is to pool the company's activities within the roles it plans to fill.

The first employees at start-ups often find themselves wearing a number of different hats. Marketers can provide customer service to the first batch of buyers. Developers may have to double as QA testers. The UX designer may also have to produce the look-and-feel of the brand, as well as determine the way the service works.

By pooling activities, start-ups are able to minimize early recruitment, while also giving those first employees a wider breadth of experience in the company's activities.

Finally, having recruited only those people who are essential to the company's services, pooled their activities into defined roles, and outsourced the rest, the company can begin augmenting the roles by assigning productivity tools to make the team members more efficient.

As that augmentation meets the limits of its efficiency, the company will then need to begin looking for new staff to meet the new demand and fill skills gaps.

Adding Skills and Structuring a Company

The challenge of recruiting good staff should never end. As the company grows, the workload faced by current employees will start to become overwhelming. A start-up will also find that it could benefit from additional activities or greater specialization. As customer growth justifies the hiring of a full-time customer service person and the rate of new commits places heavy demand on QA testing, the marketing person should be able to focus on generating new customers while a specialized customer service rep answers questions and deals with requests. The developer should be able to focus on writing code while a QA expert tries to break that code.

The presence of skills gaps will slow the growth of the company, and yet young companies often find themselves struggling to fill those spots, frequently because they don't know how to fill them. They don't know where to find people with the skills they need, how to attract them, or how to enthuse them to join the company, contribute to it—and continue contributing to it.

That's easier for some companies than for others. Some industries will always appear particularly attractive and fun to work in. The entertainment and fashion industries rarely lack competition for internships and entry-level positions. At Mdundo, Martin Nielsen has found that the appeal of working in the music industry makes recruitment easier than he expects it would be in other industries, a characteristic that he says colleagues in the music industries in the UK and Denmark have also noted.

A real Get Shit Done Team building Mdundo

Nonetheless, recruitment is not straightforward in any industry. There are multiple factors—from the identities of the founders, the investors, and the first employees to the nature of the work—that will influence how much a new company will struggle to fill its roles. Nor does the challenge end when those hires walk through the door. Companies also need structures. Teams need leaders and reporting channels. Information has to flow between departments. Every task that the company needs to perform has to be allocated so that someone is performing it—even the jobs that no one wants to do.

At the beginning of the life of a start-up, when it's made up of little more than an interesting idea and a handful of friends, that structuring is relatively straightforward. Everyone knows what's happening in the business and even if no one volunteers to do the search engine optimization or manage the server, someone will eventually agree because otherwise a necessary chore won't get done and the business will suffer.

As new recruits join the company though, the structure becomes more important. New team members who aren't co-founders can feel less invested in the company, less motivated, and need more guidance. Instead of understanding which tasks the company needs to complete, and getting on with it, they'll be more likely to wait until they're told by someone above them in the company what work they need to perform next.

At that point, structure becomes vital to ensure that work can be allocated and reviewed. But with the growth of those management structures to ensure the flow of work and responsibility come clusters which can block information flows across the company. Much of the work performed by ways of working consultants and Agile transformation experts involves breaking down the silos that prevent different teams from seeing the complete production flow.

There are no easy answers here and no set formulas to ensure that team members have both the information they need to execute their tasks and the freedom to co-ordinate with others. The ideal set-up will allow team members to learn from and communicate with other clusters in the company, be able to access information but not waste too much time in meetings, sharing knowledge and managing relationships.

Those challenges are part of the development of a start-up anywhere in the world. In sub-Saharan Africa, though, both recruitment and structure present their own challenges.

Recruitment and Management Structures in African Start-Ups

Sub-Saharan Africa has a lot of people who need work. Kenya's official unemployment rate at the end of 2019 was 4.9 percent, and 14.2 percent for people aged 20 to 24.[86] Less officially, as many as 38.9 percent of Kenyans aged between 18 and 34 could be out of work.[87] In South Africa, the official unemployment rate is 30.1 percent.[88] A great deal of talent and ability in Africa is currently wasted selling hats on the side of the road or shifting from one small, dead-end job to another. The growth of digital start-ups has the potential to create meaningful, lucrative work for people who need it, can do it, and will benefit from it.

We've already seen that the path from young talent and a youthful interest in technology to graduating with a degree in a field like software engineering in sub-Saharan Africa isn't smooth or straight. Only around 11.5 percent of Kenya's school-leavers enroll in tertiary education,[89] a figure which suggests that a great deal of talent is being left behind by an inability to pay school fees, by poor teachers, and by a threadbare education system. Worry about the skills gap that missing education creates is particularly high in Africa. Among African chief executives, 87 percent expressed concern about the lack of available skills, with almost half saying that they were "extremely concerned."[90]

---

[86] Kenya National Bureau of Statistics, *Quarterly Labour Force Report, Quarter 4, October-December 2019,* February 2020 https://www.knbs.or.ke/?p=5800

[87] Patrick Alushula, "Census: 39pc of Kenya youth are unemployed," *BusinessDailyAfrica.com*, February 24 2020, https://www.businessdailyafrica.com/economy/39pc-of-Kenya-youth-are-unemployed/3946234-5466820-prx927/index.html

[88] Stats SA, *Quarterly Labour Force Survey Quarter 1: 2020,* June 23, 2020 http://www.statssa.gov.za/publications/P0211/P02111stQuarter2020.pdf

[89] "Kenya," UNESCO, last accessed September 15, 2020 http://uis.unesco.org/en/country/ke

[90] *23rd Annual Global CEO Survey: Navigating the rising tide of uncertainty,* PwC, 2020 https://www.pwc.com/gx/en/ceo-survey/2020/reports/pwc-23rd-global-ceo-survey.pdf

Local graduates with proven abilities and good qualifications have plenty of choices and can easily find well-paid jobs in the local offices of multinationals. Their need to support their families means that the riskier environment of small start-ups can look much less attractive. So while every job vacancy will attract plenty of applications, new businesses struggle to find staff with the specific skills and the qualifications that they need. One option is word-of-mouth. Daniel Maison, the former CEO of Sky.Garden, argues that "good people know good people," which is often how start-ups find their first employees. When the developer roles needed at Sky.Garden grew beyond its founders' networks, Daniel turned first to iHub, an entrepreneur community in Nairobi for which his wife was a consultant. He outsourced work to three of iHub's developers and when he found that he clicked well with one of them, he talked with iHub about hiring the developer on a full-time basis. That developer became the CTO and one of Sky.Garden's co-founders.

A happy Sky.Garden team with Co-founder and CMO Isaac Hunja taking a group-selfie

Recruiting People and Building Partnerships in African Start-Ups

In effect, Daniel found a shortcut to assessing potential employees. He relied first on iHub's own screening process, then he was able to employ people on a short-term basis in order to see how those hires performed on the job. When one stood out, he knew he'd found gold.

The reason that taking temporary help was so valuable for Sky. Garden is that the range of abilities on offer in Africa is so broad. A business in Denmark that employs an electrician to install wiring in its factory will know that the people who turn up to work will be qualified. They might not be the best in the business, but even the worst will be good enough to get the job done. They'll have studied, qualified, and be certified. In a context of enforced regulations, licensing, and legal standards consumers can be confident that the people they hire will be capable of doing the work they're paying them to do. The range of fees they have to pay will be narrower—there are no cheap electricians in Copenhagen—but anyone they can hire can deliver what they claim to sell.

That isn't true in Africa. Hire an electrician in Nairobi and the range of fees will be much wider—and so will the range of abilities. At the lowest end, you might get a couple of guys with singed fingers who have never seen a classroom and who learned how to install wiring by watching someone else do it (which in theory could be fine). "There's always going to be someone who's willing to do the job for whatever you ask," says Martin Nielsen. "No matter what you're looking for, you can get someone to do it for five times more or five times less."

The temptation for a new business in sub-Saharan Africa then, especially one starting with a small budget, is to save money and hire the cheapest worker available. When Martin needed someone to write for Mdundo's blog, he asked around and found that he could pay someone as much as two thousand dollars a month—or he could recruit music-lovers to contribute for free. In the end, he hired a few writers for one or two hundred dollars a month but soon found that he wasn't attracting good contributors. "It was actually quite inefficient," he recalls. They lacked experience and couldn't step up.

One solution is to assume that you'll get what you pay for, and pay the most you can afford but that leaves behind opportunities for businesses to find overlooked talent, and for that talent to make the most of their abilities. People in the region often lack the connections they need to get ahead so that even the most talented don't get the chance they deserve if they don't come from wealthy, influential families. A better option is to recruit cheap, educated, and driven staff, then build and motivate them.

That generates a new challenge. For start-ups in Silicon Valley, motivating team members is a complex issue. The bait of impactful work may pull in good recruits in Silicon Valley and the promise of a lucrative exit can pull new graduates away from steady jobs at large firms, but in sub-Saharan Africa, I've found that the appeal of a future payoff is much weaker that it would be in the West. Cash now has a much bigger pull when people have responsibilities and obligations to meet today than the reward that a warrant might bring a few years down the road. It's also much harder to imagine those rewards when so few people have seen them. A programmer joining an early-stage start-up in Israel today will have grown up reading about the exits of companies like ICQ, Waze, and Mobileye. They'll have seen the pictures of those companies' happy employees in the news, and they can imagine the moment when they join them. In Kenya, in Rwanda, and in Tanzania, those pictures are much rarer. The promise of riches tomorrow is much less solid than the reality of a sibling's school fees due next week or the offer of a slightly higher salary from a different company even if it has smaller prospects.

That makes loyalty a big issue in sub-Saharan African companies. Sam, the CEO who met me in his new Mercedes at Jomo Kenyatta airport, wasn't the only senior executive at one of my companies who saw their contractual termination period as an optional inconvenience that they could ignore when a better opportunity came their way. The Commercial Director of another of my companies once sent me an email asking me to accept his formal resignation commencing immediately.

"Due to unavoidable personal circumstances. I will not be in a position to serve the notice period," he wrote.

He was at least willing to be available for phone and email enquiries "from home on a limited basis" for a week following his departure date, and would be happy to seek his own replacement "so as not to inconvenience" me. Those "unavoidable personal circumstances" turned out not to be the need to take care of a sick family member; it

Recruiting People and Building Partnerships in African Start-Ups

was the need to take over as CEO in his father's clinic. My commercial director was leaving with no notice to take care of another company.

I've had a number of people report that they'd broken their leg on the day they'd resigned so they wouldn't be able to work out their notice, and I've lost count of the number of company laptops and smartphones that were reported lost on an employee's last or second to last day.

I've even had people quit before they started work—or more accurately, forgotten to quit. They'd accepted the offer of a senior position, asked to begin in two or three months' time but disappeared a week before their start day. For some functions that can be critical.

Of course, none of this is to say that employees in other parts of the world don't look for ways out of their obligations either. Clearly, they do. In Denmark, employees tend to hand in their resignations just before the end of the month in order to limit their termination period. Staff, especially when they're about to leave, will almost always place their own benefits ahead of the company's. But in Kenya, I have seen lot of people ignore their termination period and quit right after pay day because they expect that they won't be paid for the days worked since then. As with many other issues in Africa, this is clearly a trust issue.

That lack of trust can also extend to staff who remain with the company. My former chief executive's lumber and gas station businesses weren't unusual. "Double-jobbing" is common in Africa and in a way that extends beyond an employee having a paying hobby or supplementing their income with a little moonlighting. It can take up a lot of their professional time, and it can sometimes even compete with their day job. The CEO of BeautyClick once told me that she wanted to add a product to the company's range. She went online to search for suppliers and came to the website of a wholesaler. Listed on the page was BeautyClick's own sales manager. She had been moonlighting as a sales agent and specialist, selling a product that competed with her employer to her employer's own customers.

Paul, a good friend and a successful Kenyan businessman who was born and had worked and lived in Kenya all his life but had completed an MBA partly overseas, has been a great help in understanding cultural differences and implementing mitigation measures. One night, after I realized that a quarter of BeautyClick's inventory was being taken by insiders, he warned me against being naïve. "Don't forget this is Africa," he said. "If you used to do stock-counts monthly, do them weekly. If you used to have two CCTV cameras, have five."

He shared a story about one of his employees, a worker who had been with his hair-care production company for fifteen years. Paul decided to give him an old car to make his life more comfortable. Three months later, Paul discovered that the employee was going to the warehouse at night to fill up his car, then making sales out of the car trunk during the day and keeping the money for himself.

I still have a hard time balancing the Scandinavian leadership model with the closer monitoring that the absence of trust demands in most African businesses.

Getting Shit Done in Africa

So recruiting staff in Africa requires special care. There is high unemployment and no shortage of people willing to do the work, but there's also a lack of training and reliable certification that makes hiring a gamble. Employees' attachments to companies can also be weak. Staff can leave quickly and often have second jobs—sometimes jobs that compete with their employers. To employees, the risk of future reputational or career damage from job-hopping and burned bridges is lower than the apparent risk of losing an opportunity today.

But even when you can find good staff and keep them motivated and focused, they still have to perform, and that poses yet another challenge. The problem isn't a willingness to knuckle down and work hard. Inevitably, I've had employees who have shirked off and called in sick even as their Instagram page was filling with pictures of them partying and having a good time. That's not Africa; that's youth. More common are the people who juggle two or three jobs while also taking care of their families and commuting for more than two hours in each direction to reach the office in the morning and return home.

The bigger challenge is execution and a willingness to take the initiative.

Talking to some of the female employees at BeautyClick one day, they told me how when they were children they would often stay up late

Recruiting People and Building Partnerships in African Start-Ups

at night studying. They knew that they needed their education and they wanted to pass their exams and get on.

"Sometimes," one woman told me, "I would stay up so late studying that I would fall asleep in class the next day."

"The teacher didn't mind?" I asked.

"Oh, yes," she replied, laughing. "She would take a mattress and drag it out into the sun. 'If you are tired, you can sleep here,' the teacher would tell me. And we would have to sleep there, in the hot sun!" That is pretty nasty around the equator.

Other people told me that if they gave a wrong answer in class, the teacher would give them a spoon and tell them to use it to dig up a large tree.

That's the kind of upbringing that quickly beats out initiative and risk-taking. A CEO in South Africa told me once over a dinner that whenever his company moved into a new country in Africa they would send over a "GSD" (Get Shit Done) team to ensure execution. They couldn't rely on a new, local team to show the initiative to assess the challenge, work out solutions, and implement them.

There are ways around this problem but they require solutions adapted to the environment.

In general, start-ups need to be agile and they benefit from the freedom that a lack of structure provides. Everyone does everything and knows what everyone else is doing. Decisions are made together and responsibility is shared.

A company that begins with a team of three people doesn't need structures or managers. But the more it grows, the more structure it needs and the more control it has to implement. The development of those structures destroys some value. They box team members into roles and require permission and approval before action. They can limit initiative but people know their positions and their responsibilities. They know who they report to and they know where to look to receive assignments or ask questions.

In any business there are tipping points when the freedom of a young start-up has to acquire the structure of a stable business. One of the learnings that I've picked up in Africa is that the tipping point comes much earlier there. You need to create structures and hierarchies much sooner than you might do in Europe or in Silicon Valley so that employees feel that they have a safe space in which to operate. Most employees need to know what they can do. It needs to be work that they know how to do, with clear instructions, and clear short-term incentives. As illustrated below, the value creation in an African start-up drops much faster if it has too little structure than if, on a relative scale, it has too much structure.

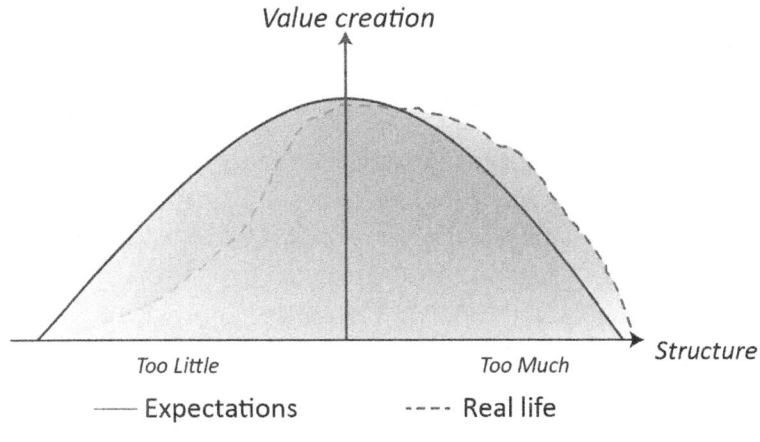

Figure 9. Illustration of structure vs. value creation

So when it comes to human resource management in sub-Saharan Africa, there are important differences. Like anywhere, a detailed recruitment process is key. Keep an eye out for double-jobbing, especially when that moonlighting affects the growth of your business (and don't be surprised if it even conflicts with the work you're paying someone to do.) Don't assume that employees will respect the provisions in their employment contracts if it's inconvenient for them to do so, and while bonuses and good salaries can help to keep your team together, don't expect them to buy loyalty. Not because they are not great people or dedicated to the business, but simply because employees often have large responsibilities that they need to meet today, and they'll take priority over a good prospect in the future.

What I've found does buy commitment and positive results though is the same thing that delivers both everywhere: a passion for the work itself. Even in sub-Saharan Africa, Mdundo is able to recruit excellent staff and keep them on board without having to pay very high salaries because those team members get to work in the music industry and be appreciated for the job they do. It's a fun niche that attracts young staff. What first attracted Daniel Maison to Sky.Garden and away from the dream job that he was doing scaling businesses—and what kept him building the company—is the impact he knows that the business is making.

Sky.Garden enables small businesses to reach far more customers than those businesses would otherwise be able to do. Some sellers have even been able to close unprofitable real-world outlets and move entirely online, generating better returns for themselves and for their families. "My best moment," says Daniel, "was when a seller told me that he didn't have to pay rent anymore."

The promise of work making a meaningful impact on people's lives motivates teams—just as it motivates investors—everywhere.

Partnerships—Teaming Up with Other African Businesses

We've seen that employee contracts can have little practical value. Both sides might agree that an employee will give a month's notice before they leave, and will return all their company equipment on their last day, but my experience is that when some team members decide it's time to go, they go.

Clearly, that poses some risk, especially when employees have access to confidential data. But it's part of the experience of doing business in Africa. You need a plan in place for someone else to step up quickly if a key employee leaves with little notice, and you have to assume that other businesses will compete for your customers—and sometimes that competition will come from inside your own company.

Another big opportunity—and risk—comes from partnerships. Businesses are rarely built alone, especially digital companies which tend to provide platforms that other companies use. Alibaba, like Amazon, didn't grow into a giant firm by buying goods from wholesalers and selling them directly to consumers. They generated large profits by partnering with other companies: Alibaba relies on its network of sellers. Alipay, part of the Alibaba Group, has partnered with Barclaycard and other payment companies to enable Chinese citizens to use its app when they make purchases abroad. That partnership makes it much easier for Alipay to continue delivering its service to Chinese tourists than to build its own payment infrastructure around the world. Partnering with other payment services has allowed it to make use of the reach those services have already built.

Partnerships like that enable companies to acquire resources that would otherwise be hard, expensive, or time-consuming to obtain. They make growth into new regions easier, and they can provide access to markets without the need to create new channels. At the end of 2019, for example, Mdundo announced a partnership with Opera Mini, Africa's second most popular browser. Mdundo would display in the browser the 100 most popular songs in the user's country. Users would then be able to stream or download them, while Opera Mini's file-sharing feature meant that they would also be able to share music without accruing data costs.

Opera Mini got to offer their users a valuable extra function without the need to sign up artists individually; Mdundo got to reach new audiences in nine sub-Saharan countries without the need to pay for marketing.

Partnerships like these work because they benefit both sides. They're effective when they're formed between complementary firms that might have a common alliance history. They should be properly governed and effectively managed. Both firms should also be committed to the relationship, which should reflect common goals that are important to both partners.

But partnerships can also fail. One side may not meet their obligations. The two partners might find that they become competitors. If Opera Mini decides to launch its own music service (or if Mdundo were to decide that it wanted to get into the browser business), the relationship between the two partners would change from co-operation to competition. Opera Mini is also trusting that Mdundo has data that reveals the most popular songs in each region; Mdundo is trusting Opera Mini to place its lists in a prominent place and continue to supply free file-sharing.

As long as both sides continue to benefit from the relationship, they'll want the partnership to continue, but any party to an agreement has to bear in mind the risks and consequences of a dispute. That might mean turning to the courts for adjudication. Amazon will have little trouble enforcing a contract in the United States. Even in China, foreign firms can enforce contracts against the wishes of local defendants. Writing in 2015, Steve Dickinson, a China law expert, noted that in the past, foreign buyers would place orders in China without contracts or any written agreements beyond specifications listed in an email exchange. "This informal approach made some sense because there was no alternative," he says.[91]

By 2015, however, the situation had changed. As long as a contract is governed by Chinese law, written in Chinese, is enforceable in a Chinese court with jurisdiction over the defendant, and is litigated in the district where the Chinese defendant has its principle place of business, that litigation is more likely to produce a good result for a foreign party than litigation in almost any other Asian court. "Litigation is not futile," writes Dickinson, "and my firm has had good success overseeing litigation in courts all over China."

There are exceptions. There's little point in trying to litigate against an organization owned by the Party, by the military or by the offspring of a Party official. But otherwise, as long as the two parties have a contract that meets China's specifications, courts will enforce it.

That isn't true yet in most of sub-Saharan Africa. A survey of 34 African countries conducted by Transparency International, an anti-corruption group, found that 46 percent of respondents believed that most or all judges and magistrates are corrupt.[92] The perception varies from country to country. In Kenya, only 28 percent of respondents thought that most or all judges and magistrates would take a bribe in 2019, a decline of five percentage points over the previous four years. In

---

[91] Steve Dickinson, "China Contracts: Make Them Enforceable Or Don't Bother," ChinaLawBlog, August 18, 2015 https://www.chinalawblog.com/2015/08/contracts-in-china-enforce-it-or-go-home.html

[92] Coralie Pring and Jon Vrushi, *Global Corruption Barometer Africa 2019*, Transparency International, July 2019 https://www.transparency.org/files/content/pages/2019_GCB_Africa.pdf

Nigeria, more than half the respondents expected a judge to be corrupt, a rise of 6 percentage points since 2015. The 72 percent of Kenyans who believe that their judicial system is mostly honest may be optimistic. In June 2020, a magistrate sentenced a court clerk to a fine of 800,000 shillings or two years in jail for accepting a bribe to influence a case. The case involved a dispute between two factions of the African Independent Pentecostal Church of Kenya. In 2019, petitioners accused four of the country's seven Supreme Court judges of accepting bribes and said that two of the judges had asked for "tens of millions of shillings" to influence a case with political significance.

It's helpful to know that in the event of a dispute with a partner, you have recourse to courts who can force partners to abide by their agreements. But in sub-Saharan Africa, start-ups have to operate without that safety net. They have to form partnerships knowing that if their partner fails to abide by the terms of the agreement, their only recourse will be their own actions.

The transparency that digitalization can bring helps. Sky.Garden buys services from delivery companies but because it's a digital firm, it doesn't have to depend on the companies' reports that they're doing a good job. It can track data and see whether the delivery firms are meeting their obligations. If packages fail to arrive or drivers take a strangely long time to reach their destinations, Sky.Garden can call it quits and send more work to a different delivery firm. Similarly, if a delivery firm sees that Sky.Garden isn't sending it the level of work it anticipates, it can pull out of the agreement.

The same transparency that Sky.Garden can apply to its suppliers can also be applied in partnerships, especially between digital firms. Mdundo can see how many extra downloads its agreement with Opera Mini is bringing it. The browser can see how many of its users are engaging with that on-screen real estate. If the benefits of the partnership start to become unbalanced, then partners can expect the relationship to start breaking down regardless of whether there's a written agreement describing the obligations of each side.

Recruiting People and Building Partnerships in African Start-Ups

Sky.Garden direct-to-consumer delivery model in short

What secures a partnership in Africa isn't the terms of a contract but a sense that both sides are benefitting. Sometimes, that might mean giving away more than a partner demands in order to safeguard the future of the relationship. The opportunity that Mdundo exploited opened because telcos in Africa were taking as much as 80 percent of the revenue generated by artists' downloads. One side of the partnership was getting much more out of the relationship than the other. Martin Nielsen has had the experience of reaching an agreement with a partner then going back and telling them that he was raising their revenue share to strengthen that partnership's stability. "I just know that over time that partner will lose motivation because their money is not going to be enough for them," he says. "I'm better off structuring it in a way where I make sure that it is going make sense for them."

Removing the safety net of an enforceable contract then can force African start-ups to think differently about how they work with other companies. The aim of a partnership between firms in sub-Saharan Africa is not to extract the maximum possible benefit from that relationship for themselves but to ensure that both sides benefit and will continue to benefit as the partnership grows. At the same time, it's also important to ensure that the partnership can break cleanly if necessary.

"It's just much more of a people thing," says Martin Nielsen, "and a much more creative partnership framework."

Building Teams and Partners in Africa Requires Creativity, Flexibility, and Patience

In the previous chapter, we looked at the development of business ideas. We looked at where ideas come from, how they're constructed, how they can be replicated, and how to turn them into business models.

But translating those ideas into business models and into thriving companies doesn't happen alone. It happens through the work of teams and through the forging of partnerships. Both of those represent both challenges and opportunities in sub-Saharan Africa.

A lack of training and certification means that despite high unemployment, particularly among youth, companies can struggle to find qualified applicants. Even when they can find them, businesses can't always expect the same degree of loyalty that they might assume they have in the US or Europe. Even top staff may leave at short notice if they see what appears to be even a slightly better opportunity elsewhere. The family obligations that many wage-earners carry means that short-term benefits can be more powerful incentives than the promise of future rewards. And those who do remain will often need closer management than you might expect, with clear areas of responsibility and management structures.

Partnerships, too, have to be formed without the safety net of enforceable legal contracts. Companies have to assume that a partnership will only last as long as it's mutually beneficial.

Despite those challenges, though, there's no shortage of advantages for recruiters and plenty of valuable partnership opportunities. Talent and ability are universal, and sub-Saharan Africa contains plenty of capable people who just need an opportunity, training, and development. The relatively low cost of living and the competition for jobs means that that talent is available for a much lower fee than almost anywhere else in the world, even as the fruits of that talent can then be sold to a continent-sized market. New employees might need more management than their counterparts in the West but that just means earlier structures and

Recruiting People and Building Partnerships in African Start-Ups

closer reviews. Done carefully, businesses can find that they're able to capitalize on one of Africa's most valuable assets: its human resources.

And while businesses can't depend on courts to enforce partnership contracts, any recourse to the courts represents a failure of a relationship. Partnerships in Africa may be higher risk but they have to be planned the way that partnerships should always be planned: as agreements between parties who have value to offer each other.

All of that makes working in Africa complex, challenging but also exciting and rewarding. It suggests that the region can have a great future. That's what I'll discuss in the next chapter.

Chapter Seven

The Future of Sub-Saharan Africa—and Why It's Not Here Now

We often talk about the potential of sub-Saharan Africa. We look to the future for its prosperity and imagine the smart mega-cities filled with innovative tech companies and the middle- and high-earners that will one day make up the capitals of Kenya, Nigeria, and Tanzania.

We have to talk about "potential" and the "future" because despite the abundant availability of human resources and the new penetration of digital technology, none of those things make up Africa's present now. Both Lagos and Shanghai have about 20 million people but while Shanghai has the world's second tallest building and sixteen subway lines covering more than 700 kilometers, Lagos is still building its first metro line, ten years after its anticipated completion date. The Nigerian city is better known for its corrugated iron shacks than for its glass and steel skyscrapers. China's unemployment rate in 2019 was about 3.6 percent and its GDP per capita crossed $10,000 that year. The World Bank puts the unemployment rate of sub-Saharan Africa at a little over 6 percent, although those figures are highly optimistic and don't count the region's massive underemployment. Sub-Saharan Africa's GDP per capita in 2019 was less than $1,600.[93]

So why do analysts continue to talk optimistically about Africa's future? Why, having seen the region plod into the twenty-first century,

---

[93] "Unemployment, total (% of total labor force) (modeled ILO estimate – Sub-Saharan Africa," The World Bank, data retrieved in June 21, 2020 https://data.worldbank.org/indicator/SL.UEM.TOTL.ZS?locations=ZG

instead of conquering it, do investors still see sub-Saharan Africa as a region of opportunity?

Part of the reason is hope. It's been only fifteen years since China's GDP per capita was at the same level as sub-Saharan Africa's is now in current prices.[94] In that time, the country has become the world's manufacturing center, sucked rural workers away from unproductive farms into the cities to churn out jeans and socks at low prices, then transformed into a high-tech factory that produces iPhones and smart televisions by the million. It's now an innovation hub in its own right.

China has shown the world that when the conditions for change are present that change can happen remarkably fast. If a country in sub-Saharan Africa were to follow the trajectory of China, by 2035 it would be a middle-income nation. If all the countries in the region were to follow that path, the continent would be transformed. Hundreds of millions would be lifted out of poverty. Investors who put their money in now would have the dual satisfaction of knowing that they had helped to bring about a transformation that improved millions of people's lives, and they would also be able to enjoy the financial rewards that come with that kind of growth. Clearly, China's growth is based on a policy and a path that has been heavily debated. It's not clear whether any country could or should replicate it, but in regards to creating an impactful transformation the economic results of China could be a guiding star.

There are few places in the world that promise investors so much impact and so much potential reward for their effort.

Two of what appear to be the most powerful conditions for that transformation are already in place. We've already seen that Africa has one of the world's youngest populations. About sixty percent of Africa's 1.25 billion people are under the age of 25.[95] By 2050, 362 million Africans

---

[94] GDP per capita (current US$) – China, The World Bank, last accessed September 15, 2020, 2020 https://data.worldbank.org/indicator/NY.GDP.PCAP.CD?locations=CN

[95] Fred Dews, "Charts of the Week: Africa's changing demographics," Brookings, January 18, 2020

https://www.brookings.edu/blog/brookings-now/2019/01/18/charts-of-the-week-africas-changing-demographics/

will be aged between 15 and 24.[96] As China ages and its working age population shrinks, a result of years of strict population control, Africa is becoming increasingly youthful, populated by young people who use their smartphones to send and receive money, to upload pictures of their parties to Instagram, to read and share news, and to stay in touch with their contacts across the continent. In short, they use their mobile devices in largely the same way that young people anywhere in the world use them. Like the rest of the world, they have global knowledge in their pockets and can enjoy all the benefits that today's connectivity has brought the world.

It's that combination of youth and digital nativehood that continues to so excite investors and analysts. African prosperity might be far behind much of the rest of the world but it has both the people and the digital technology the people need to build start-ups, roll out new technologies, and move the continent forward rapidly.

And yet that movement doesn't seem to be happening rapidly at all. Africa may be moving forward but instead of racing through the twenty-first century at digital speed, it's dawdling and tripping over obstacles. African technology unicorns are still as rare as white rhinos.

So what's going wrong? Why isn't sub-Saharan Africa living up to its hype? Why isn't that potent combination of a youthful population armed with the latest technology not propelling forward a continent that has so much distance to make up?

Young, Poorly Educated, and Armed with $40 Mobile Phones

Part of the problem is down to that initial impression. Sub-Saharan Africa may have almost half a billion mobile subscribers but, as we've seen, data remains expensive and the devices that people use tend to be relatively simple. Apple has 42 retail stores in China, seven in Shanghai

---

[96] John Page, "How industries without smokestacks can address Africa's youth unemployment crisis," Brookings, January 11, 2019
https://www.brookings.edu/research/how-industries-without-smokestacks-can-address-africas-youth-unemployment-crisis/

alone; it has none in Africa. The most popular smartphone in Kenya in 2019 was The Neon, a phone that cost 3,999 KES, less than $40. Safaricom sold 600,000 units of the phone that year. The most popular phone manufacturer in Kenya is Transsion, a Chinese company little known in the West, that sells brands like Tecno and Infinix.

It may be true to speak of digital penetration in sub-Saharan Africa but while digital technology has reached much of the region and spread widely, it hasn't penetrated deeply. Many of the benefits that digitalization promises are lost when users have to count their megabytes because they can't afford constant connectivity, and when half a gigabyte of internal memory means that they can barely download apps.

Having access to a smartphone is not the same as having access to all of the benefits that smartphones and digitalization can bring. If customers aren't using the latest processors and don't have access to affordable data, entrepreneurs in Africa will struggle to replicate ideas from other markets or build new products. The solutions that they offer will have to be much more limited if targeting the mass market and are likely to be less profitable.

And just as the idea of Africa's digital penetration has been overrated, so too are the benefits of the region's young population. There is certainly a huge amount of potential in the continent. There is no shortage of ability and drive. I've been lucky enough to find and employ executives, managers, and staff who would succeed and rise to the top of any company anywhere in the world. Africans have the capacity to drive the continent forward.

But they can't do that without education—and that's one of the biggest problems holding the continent back. According to UNESCO, sub-Saharan Africa has the world's highest rate of education exclusion. More than one-fifth of children between the ages of 6 and 11 are out of school, and a third of children between the ages of about 12 and 14. Only 40 percent of young people between the ages of 15 and 17 are in education.[97] Nine out of ten adolescents lack basic skills in reading and

---

[97] "Education in Africa," UNESCO, last accessed September 15, 2020 http://uis.unesco.org/en/topic/education-africa

arithmetic. Tertiary education enrollment in the region is just 9.4 percent. The global average is 38 percent.[98]

Those who do have the opportunity to attend university can expect crowded classrooms and often poor teaching. Young people with the talent and the ability to build the businesses that sub-Saharan Africa needs are cut off from the skills and knowledge they need to build those companies. Only a few can afford to go to university and the luckiest, who are able to go to good universities, are more likely to take secure jobs in multinationals than choose the riskier path of entrepreneurialism, especially if they have family obligations to fulfill, as many do.

The result is that while sub-Saharan Africa has a young population, the region's governments have largely done too little to equip that population with the skills they need to transform the region, and the environment in which they can take risks to put those skills to use.

Other regions struggle with education too. China's tertiary education system is neither perfect nor perfectly fair. While over 90 percent of students from large cities in China attend senior high school, only half of all junior high graduates in poor, rural areas achieve the same education level.[99] The qualifications needed to attend the best universities vary from region to region, leading some analysts to describe Chinese colleges as "a rich, Han, urban, male club."[100] And yet according to China's Ministry of Education, 276 million students were enrolled in degree-granting institutions in 2018, a 2 percent increase from the previous year.[101] One

---

[98] *COVID-19 Coronavirus Response: Tertiary Education in Sub-Saharan Africa*, The World Bank, June 16, 2020 http://pubdocs.worldbank.org/en/109901592405885723/One-Africa-TE-and-Covid-06162020.pdf

[99] Yaojiang Shi, Linxiu Zhang, Yue Ma, Hongmei Yi, Chengfang Liu, Natalie Johnson, James Chu, Prashant Loyalka and Scott Rozelle (2015). Dropping Out of Rural China's Secondary Schools: A Mixed-methods Analysis. *The China Quarterly*, 224, pp 1048–1069 doi:10.1017/S0305741015001277

[100] Anning Hu (2014). Reassessing Disparity in Access to Higher Education in Contemporary China. *The China Quarterly*, 220, pp 1123-1130 doi:10.1017/S0305741014001167

[101] *Overview of educational achievements in China in 2018*, Ministry of Education, The People's Republic of China, October 22, 2019 http://en.moe.gov.cn/documents/reports/201910/t20191022_404775.html

reason that China has managed to transform itself and its economy is that it has established pathways to education for its young people. It may not be making the most of its human resources but it is making a great deal out of them. That still isn't true in sub-Saharan Africa.

So those two key factors that suggest so much promise for sub-Saharan Africa are weaker than they appear, and they make building start-ups in the region difficult. Africa's digital penetration is not as technologically advanced as it needs to be to have the impact the region needs. Clearly, this is changing day by day. Data is growing cheaper. The average phone is becoming better and the networks are improving drastically. 2Africa, for example, a project whose backers include Facebook, is one of the largest subsea cable projects in the world and will connect 23 countries in Africa, the Middle East, and Europe. The area might also have a young population but if that population isn't being educated, their potential will be wasted.

The weakness of those two foundations mean that sub-Saharan Africa can't move as quickly as it should. But even where it is moving, even when African graduates with drive and digital skills are building businesses, they're still running into a number of obstacles.

Where's the Money?

The first is the funding, a problem that I've seen time and time again. There's only so much that accelerators and individual investors who want their capital to have an impact can do. We can assess ideas and give entrepreneurs the fuel they need to get started. We can use our experience to give them advice. We can use our connections to introduce them to people who can help and partners who can help them grow. But the power of individual investors to scale a small African start-up is limited. That kind of change, the movement from proving a concept to conquering a market, requires far more funding than is generally available to entrepreneurs in sub-Saharan Africa. Entrepreneurs can come up with great ideas, great traction, prepare perfect PowerPoint pitches, and meet the right people, and still come away with only just enough funding to make their first hires.

The result is that the pattern of growth for sub-Saharan African start-ups is very different to that of start-ups in other parts of the world. Local companies have to move quickly towards profitability. They can't spend years buying market share in the way that companies like Uber and Amazon have done. They can't burn through venture capital funds as they test ideas, run betas, and push out minimal viable products so that when they do turn to profitability, they're already dominant. If they can't show that they can survive on their own terms within a short time, they won't survive at all.

That makes it difficult enough for a start-up to grow quickly into a unicorn despite the potential for a technology firm to reach a large market. But in sub-Saharan Africa, the alternative path to growth—the slow accumulation of a paying customer base—is difficult too. Digital entrepreneurs in sub-Saharan Africa know that the market they're aiming at will have limited buying power and be reluctant to pay for digital products and services. Customers using a $40 smartphone and paying for data as they go are unlikely to pay a subscription fee for online storage or for access to content.

That obstacle can sometimes be overcome by adjusting business plans and altering the product. Spotify sells streaming subscriptions; Mdundo gives free, ad-supported downloads. But it means that sub-Saharan African entrepreneurs have two difficulties: they don't have the funds to build a big business or subsidize a free trial; but they also don't have an easy market from which to scoop up paying customers.

What a Lack of Trust Can Do

One of the most striking things about doing business in sub-Saharan Africa is the lack of trust. Buyers don't trust sellers to always deliver quality goods. Sellers don't trust buyers to always pay what they owe. Employees don't trust employers to always pay their salaries and employers don't trust employees to always work out their contracts and dedicate themselves to the firm. They may *hope* that the seller turns out to be trustworthy, the buyer honest, the employer responsible, and the employee dedicated—and usually they are—but no one in sub-Saharan Africa is surprised when they aren't.

Sellers will often have to compete with rivals who have skipped the heavy customs duty on their goods. Buyers may find that they've run out of funds before the bill becomes due. Employers operating on a shoestring budget may need only one deal to go sour to be unable to meet payroll, and employees with student debts and family obligations would rather burn a bridge than lose a better opportunity.

And customers are right to be distrustful even when they're buying brands. In August 2020, an investigation by BuzzFeed News and Secure-D, a mobile security service, found malware embedded in Transsion's phones.[102] The programs, xHelper and Triada, would generate pop-up ads during calls and texts. They also downloaded apps and tried to subscribe users to paid services without their knowledge. Users would find that their pre-paid data was drying up much faster than they'd expected.

The malware wasn't the result of customers downloading apps from unreliable sources. They appear to have been installed when the phones were manufactured in China, and couldn't be removed even with a factory reset. When your experience of buying low-cost brands is that negative, the result will be a weakening of trust in purchases as a whole—and a greater challenge for start-ups trying to build brands of their own.

All of that lack of trust makes doing business in sub-Saharan Africa harder than in many other regions of the world. It requires extraordinary contingency plans—payment in advance or on delivery; an employee ready for promotion if a key executive suddenly leaves. But there is another area in which trust is also low: sub-Saharan Africans have little reason to trust their governments.

Taxes in Denmark are high. Income taxes reach more than 55 percent but we know where those taxes are going. Citizens might disagree about the tax rate and how to spend those taxes, but there are no surprises. We know exactly how much we need to pay, and how those taxes are set. We know what we need to do if we want to change the tax rates,

---

[102] Craig Silverman, "Secretly Stealing Money from People Around the World," *BuzzFeed News*, August 24, 2020 https://www.buzzfeednews.com/article/craigsilverman/cheap-chinese-smartphones-malware

and we know that the government isn't going to suddenly remember a tax it hasn't levied and apply it retroactively on a successful business that's winning attention.

That isn't true in sub-Saharan African countries. Kresten Buch, one of the founders of accelerator 88mph, has argued that the complexity of Africa's laws make it almost impossible for a company not to break the law.

"I've had cases where you don't understand how much you actually should pay in tax," he recalled. "Then the government official comes. You broke the law. Now you need to pay."

When I started BeautyClick, IFU advised me that the chances that a government official will turn up holding a retroactive tax bill increase as the company grows. The more successful the company becomes, and the more money it appears to make, the more taxes a government and government officials will find to levy against it. Successful businesses have no objection to paying taxes but they need to know what taxes they have to pay so that they can plan their finances accordingly.

Entrepreneurs in Africa can't trust governments not to surprise them with new demands—and they certainly can't trust them to spend what they take on social benefits such as education. Again, that kind of risk acts as a disincentive to the entrepreneurial efforts that the region needs.

Africa Needs More Africans To Come Home, And More Immigrants to Come

It also acts as a disincentive to expats and immigrants. One of the biggest challenges that sub-Saharan Africans face is that so many of its best and brightest, the people it sends to universities abroad, want to stay abroad where they'll earn more, enjoy a higher standard of living, and have a greater chance to fulfill their potential.

Some countries facing the same problem have rolled out programs to draw their citizens home. China's Thousand Talents Plan offers signing bonuses, housing support, children's education, "returnee parks" and other bonuses to persuade *haigui*—a play on words for citizens who repatriate that can mean both "sea turtles" and "returning home"—to bring their skills and training back to China. Israel's Returning Residents can enjoy benefits that include discounted flights, income support on arrival, a reduced tax rate on a car purchase, a ten-year tax exemption on income earned abroad, as well as job placement for returning scientists and loans for returning entrepreneurs.

But those programs always have to compete with the benefits of continuing to work elsewhere in the world. In 2018, China claimed that it had managed to attract about 500,000 of its citizens back to the country but those figures may be questionable.[103] According to the Brookings Institution, 90 percent of Chinese students who had earned an American Ph.D. in artificial intelligence between 2014 and 2018 chose to remain in the US. Many returnees have come to regret their decision and returned abroad, creating a new term: *huihai*, or "returning overseas."

Skilled professionals who can work in places with higher pay and better prospects won't be coming home and staying home until their countries of origin can offer comparable benefits. African countries, then, might hope that they can stem or at least reduce their brain drain, but as long as other countries can offer more lucrative rewards there's little they can do to stop or reverse it. What they can do though is make it easier for people who do want to live and work in the region to do so.

From applying and paying for visas to obtaining residency to withholding taxes, sub-Saharan African countries throw up obstacle after obstacle to expats and immigrants who want to invest and work in their countries. Those obstacles put off and keep out exactly the kind of dynamic, entrepreneurial people the countries need to build businesses and create local jobs.

Moving to a city like Kinshasa or Lagos isn't an easy decision but the people who are willing to make that move are energetic and driven. They're the kind of people who make things happen—as Israel, the Start-up Nation made up of immigrants, has found.

Clearing away the tax and visa obstacles that make moving to and between sub-Saharan African countries so difficult isn't a huge task. It

---

[103] Remco Zwetsloot, "China's Approach To Tech Talent Competition: Policies, Results, And The Developing Global Response," *Global China: Assessing China's Growing Role in the World,* April 2020

https://www.brookings.edu/wp-content/uploads/2020/04/FP_20200427_china_talent_policy_zwetsloot.pdf requires planning and policymaking, some of which is already underway, but until it happens more broadly, those countries will struggle to replace the talent they lose abroad each year, and start-ups will continue struggle to find the talent they need to create their companies.

Steer Clear of the Courts

Finally, entrepreneurs building start-ups in the West quickly become used to dealing with lawyers. They need lawyers to draw up investment agreements, shareholder agreements, partnership agreements, create employment contracts, etc.

Ideally, those contracts will be negotiated, signed, then never used. Each party knows what they're supposed to do and fulfills their obligations. But the existence of the contract increases confidence and lowers risk. An investor putting money into a new business will know that if the founders spend all the money on a new car and a big house instead of a top developer and advertising, they can turn to the courts. They don't expect that they'll have to use the courts, but they know it's an option that reduces the risk of the investment.

Non-disclosure agreements make it easier for companies to give employees access to confidential data and proprietary technology because those employees know that the courts can impose penalties if they betray that trust.

In December 2015, Anthony Levandowski, a key engineer in Google's autonomous car project, searched Google's internal repository for files relating to the project. He installed special software to access the data then downloaded 14,000 files. Two months later, he quit Google and set up his own autonomous trucking firm. Six months later, he sold the firm to Uber for $680 million.

Waymo, the self-driving car company that spun out of Google, turned to the courts. In March 2020, a San Francisco County court ordered Levandowski to pay his former employer $179 million in compensation for unfair competition and for breaching his legal obligations. Levandowski has declared bankruptcy.

It's not impossible to imagine an African court giving a company (and especially not one the size of Google) the same kind of protection from unscrupulous employees that an American court gave the search company but it is in some countries difficult. Creating a start-up is always high risk but without a reliable, trustworthy court system, the risks that start-ups face are even higher. They don't stop investors and entrepreneurs trying to build companies but they do make it harder for them to do so, and they make it more likely that money will stay away and good, impactful ideas won't be built.

Building the Future

It's easy to look at sub-Saharan Africa from the distance of Europe or the US and see a young, vibrant region ready to achieve growth at breakneck speed. It's easy to feel excitement at the potential and passion for the impact that growth will bring.

It's also easy to overrate the historical economical growth and underestimate the challenges that have to be overcome in order to realize that potential.

It's much harder at that distance to see the obstacles that still stand in the way of that growth, and to realize how much further back sub-Saharan Africa stands from the digitalization it needs if it's going to follow the path of countries like China.

But while the distance that the region needs to travel are large, and the challenges huge and complex, they can be overcome—or at least reduced so that growth can happen faster. In the next and final chapter, I'll share my view on what needs to be prioritized for sub-Saharan Africa to be able to make the most of its potential.

Conclusion

Digitalizing Africa

It's hard not to feel passion for sub-Saharan Africa. It's difficult to see a region filled with so much potential and not look forward to the explosive growth that its people could unleash, that they deserve, and that they've waited so long to enjoy.

But it's also hard to feel optimistic about the chances that that potential will be fully released any time soon. This is not to say that sub-Saharan Africa has not improved or that it will not improve at all over the next decades and become a better place to live. But the potential is so much bigger.

In the previous chapter, I explained why I believe sub-Saharan Africa's promise has still not been fulfilled. I explained why I believe that people tend to underestimate the region's potential but overestimate its development stage, and I outlined the obstacles that I've found standing in the way of the region's entrepreneurs and the difficulties that reduce growth rates that might otherwise be rivaling China's.

Some of those problems have existed for decades and they may take decades to resolve. Africa's education systems are not going to reach every child overnight and give each child the education they're entitled to any time soon. It's a complex problem whose difficulties include a lack of good teachers, missing funding, and inadequate infrastructure. There's no shortage of non-profits large and small—Build Africa, the Foundation for African Children Education, Seeds of Africa to name but three—who are all trying to improve the region's education systems. They may help individual children, which is certainly worthwhile, but building better schools across Africa, staffed with trained teachers, and ensuring that every child can attend is work for generations. It's not a problem that foreign governments, investors, or non-profits can fix entirely or quickly. There's a limit to what outsiders can do.

Similarly, outsiders, with all the goodwill in the world, can't fix sub-Saharan Africa's governance problems. Donors can pressure and nudge. They can use leverage to push improvements and increase accountability. They can demand transparency and their efforts can help to reduce corruption and increase trust, but driving corruption out of African governance is a long-term project that requires a change in governing cultures. It may happen, eventually, and some countries are doing better than others. The Corruption Perception Index produced by Transparency International, an anti-corruption group, placed Botswana 34th out of 198 countries in 2019 with a score double the regional average.[104] That ranking put it above countries such as Israel, South Korea, Italy, and Greece. But the region's average as a whole hadn't changed over the previous twelve months.

Regardless of what investors and foreign governments do and demand, many of sub-Saharan Africa's biggest problems aren't going to disappear in the near future.

But there are things that we can do to make meaningful improvements now.

DFIs Need to Broaden Their Funding Strategy

The first, and most important, is to increase funding for sub-Saharan African entrepreneurs.

According to the Association of European Development Finance Institutions, a group of fifteen European DFIs, its members now have around €15 billion invested in 1,574 African projects.[105] Those investments reach thousands of companies, the organization says, and fund banks across the continent. Almost a third of the investments goes to the financial sector but much of the rest goes to energy infrastructure, particularly renewable energy solutions, which takes 22 percent of the funding; to industry and manufacturing which takes 11 percent; and to agribusiness, which takes 8 percent.

---

[104] "Corruption Perceptions Index," Transparency International, last accessed September 15, 2020 https://www.transparency.org/en/cpi/2019

[105] "A call for action to European governments and their Development Finance Institutions - Saving jobs in Africa," eDFI, April 30, 2020 https://www.edfi.eu/news/callforaction/

Conclusion—Digitalizing Africa

There's nothing wrong with those investments. Sub-Saharan African countries need to increase their electricity supplies, and it would be good if they could do it without fossil fuels. Agriculture remains a key sector in the region, so investing in more efficient production and processes will ensure that farmers can win more returns for their effort. Mining, and the ports to ship the refined ores, all give people jobs and ensure that the countries can tap their natural resources and generate revenue.

Those are the sorts of projects that have helped sub-Saharan Africa to maintain an average growth rate of around 3.5 percent between 2010 and 2019. But that rate isn't much higher than the 2.7 percent population growth rate over the same period, and it's less than half of China's average 7.7 percent growth rate during those years.

If development finance institutions want to help sub-Saharan Africa to grow faster than its current sluggish rate and emulate countries like China and India that started in similar positions less than three decades ago, then they're going to need to change their strategy. Their current approach is not delivering the impact that Africa needs and it's not producing the growth that the region is capable of generating.

The role of DFIs is to put capital in places that the private sector won't supply with enough liquidity and so permit a higher level of economic activity than would otherwise be possible . Currently, one of those places includes sub-Saharan technology firms. Venture capital funds are good at assessing technology projects, and they know how to diversify their holdings so that if just one project in ten comes good, it pays for the losses on the other nine. They expect many of the projects they fund to fail.

But VC funds have less experience assessing the kinds of specific risks that operating in sub-Saharan Africa can bring. They don't know how to add the tax complications, hiring difficulties, and legal issues to the risks that they're used to assessing when they determine whether a tech idea is viable, its team capable, and the market amenable. They don't know the customer base and they don't know its limitations. Even though many VC partners talk about Africa as the next step and we have seen more VC entries over the last three or four years, private VC money still largely stays away from Africa.

But it's those investments that are going to transform the continent. It's those digital products and services that will bring the transparency the region needs to build trust. Only technology can scale and transform lives at breakneck speed—as we've already seen during the spread of digital money, a tool that has altered the way much of the continent does business, helps relatives, and pays for transactions.

But that impact needs funding. Technology firms need capital so that they can focus on long-term growth instead of short-term profits. They need funds to move ideas from MVPs to competitive products. And they need investments to fertilize multiple seeds so that entrepreneurs with viable ideas can try to make them work, gain experience if they don't, and still be able to try again.

DFIs should aim to foster the private sector by accepting the country risk on top of early, stage high risk projects and filling the funding gap. That's the role of a DFI: to accept risk that others won't and to foster the private sector.

To take on that role, DFIs first have to accept that they need to change their strategy. They need to add to their traditional energy, agriculture, and infrastructure projects higher risk digital projects. They should earmark more funding for govtech projects which can support the tech eco-system and at the same time help governments build the digital infrastructure that the continent needs. They need to replicate in that digital space the investment approach taken by venture capital funds. For venture capitalists, diversification is everything. While a private equity fund with a couple of hundred million dollars might invest in ten or fifteen companies, a venture capital fund would put the same amount in a portfolio of 40–80 companies to spread risk.

For DFIs, building that strategy might mean the addition of funding capacity, but not necessarily. According to Fundz, an organization that tracks funding rounds, the mean average of series A funding in 2020 was $15.6 million.[106] The median amount though was just $6.7 million; a small number of biotech investments had pushed up the mean. If we

---

[106] "Series A, B, C Funding: 2020 Averages, Investors, Valuations," Fundz, last updated August 29, 2020 https://www.fundz.net/what-is-series-a-funding-series-b-funding-and-more

exclude biotech investments, which are not yet big in Africa, and use the median figure, moving 50 African start-ups beyond seed funding and towards scaling would cost just $335 million—and of course, that money goes a lot further in sub-Saharan Africa than it does in Silicon Valley. That amount, less than 2 percent of current European DFI investment would be sufficient to set up a high-risk VC fund that could support as many as 50 African tech ventures.

That fund would need specialized management: people with the knowledge and experience to assess technology ideas as well as country risk. But that talent is available and can be drawn from both private VC funds and from DFIs.

Such a shift would require a change in the DFI culture, a greater willingness to accept losses, see projects fail and make their money back on fewer very successful cases—which always happens in the technology space. But the impact will be far greater than DFIs are producing now. A portfolio of 50 African tech companies has a good chance of producing at least one unicorn which will not only fund more investments but could deliver the kind of life-changing technology that has already transformed payments on the continent. Nor are funds spent on companies that fail wasted. They give young entrepreneurs a chance to test their ideas, employ teams, and build experience. DFIs can't build Africa's education system, but by funding start-ups they do create training centers for tech entrepreneurs in the same way that Silicon Valley's accelerators enable investors and founders to share their knowledge. Some of the funding will produce successful, high impact businesses. All of it will build an African hi-tech eco-system.

And as some start-ups succeed, other entrepreneurs also get to see entrepreneurial role models who can affirm their decisions. That's important too.

Build Young Entrepreneurial Role Models

An entrepreneur who starts a business in America may dream of being the next Bill Gates. Or the next Mark Zuckerberg. Or the next Steve Jobs. Or the next…the list is long. American tech entrepreneurs aren't just business moguls. They're also household names so that whether someone wants to build a software company, a hardware firm, or a digital services business they always have a role model to follow. They know what success in their field looks like and they can see that it's attainable. If Brian Chesky and his friends from design school can build a multi-billion dollar business by renting out a room in their San Francisco apartment then anyone can build a multi-billion dollar business. You don't need a Harvard degree in computer science or a doctorate from MIT. You don't even need a garage.

Israeli entrepreneurs might not have the same name recognition (except perhaps WeWork's Adam Neumann) but the companies do. Brands like Mobileye and Waze are universally known, and in a tech environment as close-knit as Israel's, entrepreneurs soon get to know other entrepreneurs, both those who have succeeded in the past and those who are striving now. The country has a supportive eco-system that provides both role models and mentoring.

In China too, entrepreneurs like Liu Chuanzhi, founder of Lenovo, Ma Huateng, founder of Tencent, and of course, Jack Ma, founder of AliBaba, are all familiar faces and familiar stories. Jack Ma's rise from English teacher to China's richest man through hard work and drive is now almost a national myth, a promise to Chinese youth that if they set a goal, work hard, and dedicate themselves, they can achieve anything.

Each of those entrepreneurs has created paths for others to follow. Whoever comes after them knows where they're going, what they need to do to get there, and what the destination looks like. Even more importantly, they can also see that there really is a destination that will make the sacrifice and the difficulties of the journey worthwhile.

That isn't yet the case in sub-Saharan Africa. Jumia, perhaps Africa's best known tech start-up, was founded by two French former McKinsey associates. Elon Musk, Africa's most successful tech entrepreneur, achieved his success—and continues his success—outside the continent. Even Olugbenga Agboola, the Lagos-born co-founder of Flutterwave, studied and worked abroad before setting up a fintech company. It's difficult for entrepreneurial youth in sub-Saharan Africa to see role models that they can copy, and feel assured that the goals they've set themselves are achievable. In an interview with *Africa Business Insight*, Agboola was asked if there

Conclusion — Digitalizing Africa

was anything he wishes he'd known about entrepreneurship before he started. "Oh my God," he replies, "maybe I should have taken that Microsoft job and be like my friends right now who are SVPs and making ridiculous amounts of money!"[107]

That route up a career ladder towards a well-paid vice president's position will always look easier than a risk-filled entrepreneurial path that involves fundraising, recruiting, building a product, and attempting to win customers and close deals. But having mused about a regular job in a large company with a clear career path, Agboola then states that it's been a "great," "challenging" journey and that if he were to go back in time, he would still choose an entrepreneurial path. It's the sort of conclusion that just about every entrepreneur would have said: that the path is difficult; the alternative is probably easier; but they wouldn't have it any other way.

Young African entrepreneurs need to hear about that journey. They need to see that it is a journey that's possible to make and that while it's difficult and requires sacrifices, the rewards make it worthwhile. The problem at the moment is that too few African entrepreneurs have completed it and reaped those rewards to show the value of that effort. Too few have made a journey like Jack Ma's, starting with next to nothing and, powered by curiosity and passion, built a multi-billion dollar local business.

Building up the role models that Africa *has* produced, and highlighting the path of entrepreneurialism, isn't impossible. Just as Mo Ibrahim uses awards to encourage good governance, so a number of prizes are also available to help Africa's entrepreneurs overcome those obstacles and make the most of the continent's opportunities. In Nigeria, the Ministry of Finance, Ministry of Communication Technology, and Ministry of Youth Development work with the Department for International Development and the World Bank to run the Youth Enterprise With Innovation in Nigeria program (YouWiN!). The competition awards prizes typically worth about $50,000 to entrepreneurs with the best business plans.

---

[107] Staff writer, "The journey so far: Olugbenga Agboola, CEO, Flutterwave," *How We Made It In Africa: Africa Business Insight*, January 8, 2020 https://www.howwemadeitinafrica.com/the-journey-so-far-olugbenga-agboola-ceo-flutterwave/64034/

Jack Ma, founder of Chinese Internet giant Alibaba, runs his own African entrepreneurial contest. The Africa Netpreneur Prize Initiative shares $1 million among ten African entrepreneurs. In 2019, applications numbered nearly 10,000 from 50 African countries. A Dragon's Den-type final requires the entrepreneurs to pitch their ideas to a panel of judges including Jack Ma, Strive Masiyiwa, the founder and executive chairman of Econet Group, and Ibukun Awosika, the chairman of the First Bank of Nigeria. Winners have included Nigeria's Temie Giwa-Tubosun, founder and CEO of LifeBank, and Dr. Omar Sakr, the founder and CEO of Nawah-Scientific.

Other organizations are handing out expertise to entrepreneurs instead of money. The Grow Movement matches entrepreneurs in Uganda, Malawi, and Rwanda with volunteer consultants around the world. The volunteers agree to take part in twelve remote mentoring sessions over six months. It's a little like a *consultants sans frontiers* for the business world. Mentees work in industries from craft and fashion to tourism to food processing. The organization claims that it has created 1,782 jobs and impacted nearly 50,000 people between 2010 and March 31, 2020.

Not all African entrepreneurs need that kind of help, and prizes and training are no replacement for good governance and fair taxation. But some people are aware of both the opportunities and the obstacles in Africa and want to help entrepreneurs find one and avoid the other.

In the absence of African role models, these kinds of contests can show African entrepreneurs that their efforts and sacrifices are appreciated and admired. They show young entrepreneurs that their desire to start a business isn't unique or unusual, that it can be pursued, and that it's worth pursuing. Once Africa has produced its own Jeff Bezos or created an Elon Musk who studies and remains in a sub-Saharan African country, the need for such contests will be less important. Until then though, investors and brands can sponsor more competitions like the Africa Netpreneur Prize Initiative. The amounts aren't large. The Africa Netpreneur Prize Initiative offers a share of a prize worth a million dollars; one million dollars is a lot of money, but in the bigger picture that funding could be easily be increased and spread widely. Competitions could be limited to countries or regions, by industry, and by product

Conclusion — Digitalizing Africa

type. Each award gives entrepreneurs not just funding to help them continue moving forward but also a small achievement that shows that they're on the right track and that their sacrifices are worthwhile.

Entrepreneurs who have seen success, built companies, and exited can also be encouraged to take public roles and act as mentors to groups of young entrepreneurs.

It's always hard to build a business but as we've seen, it's particularly hard in sub-Saharan Africa where graduates usually have family obligations that have to be met today and can't wait until after the IPO or the buyout. The creation of more entrepreneurial role models won't remove those obligations. Nor will it remove the obstacles of weak courts, difficult recruitment, and markets with little spare cash. But it is something that's doable now, and it can give encouragement to young African business-builders wondering whether to take a challenging, difficult journey or choose the easier route to the senior vice president's office.

Let Them In

Finally, there's little that African countries can do to blunt the appeal of the West to its brightest and its most dynamic. As long as the US and Europe continue to offer good education, opportunities, and a high standard of living, young Africans fortunate enough to be able to make the most of those opportunities will try to do so.

But sub-Saharan African countries do have plenty to offer themselves: vibrant cities, incredible natural resources, and the potential for dramatic growth. Just as countries like China and Israel have taken measures to encourage their citizens to return and build local businesses, so African countries too should be formulating packages for their citizens to return.

The elements that those packages need will vary from country to country. Taxation will be one aspect. Countries don't have to go as far as Israel's policy of not collecting tax on foreign income for ten years but they can offer other tax incentives to make moving to the country inviting. Kenya's corporation tax rate, for example, is 30 percent. In Denmark, a country characterized by high personal income tax, corporation tax is just 22 percent. Lowering corporation tax in general, and specifically for returning citizens or foreign investors, would be one relatively easy way for Kenya to make growing businesses in the country more attractive, and bring in additional foreign investment.

African countries can also make work permits easier for foreigners and investors to obtain, and they can streamline bureaucratic procedures so that obtaining those permits and setting up local businesses is faster and less onerous.

African countries should be looking for measures that attract investors and entrepreneurs, instead of putting up the kinds of barriers that only those with the greatest passion for the region will attempt to hurdle. Foreign governments can help by leveraging the aid and loans they supply to push African countries to reduce taxes on new immigrants and returning citizens, and give Africa the immigration it needs to grow.

Building a New Future in Sub-Saharan Africa

Compared to the difficulties that sub-Saharan Africa faces, spreading funding to the technology sector, developing entrepreneurial role models, and paving the way for more immigration look like small measures. They won't build Africa's missing education system, create efficient government, or produce reliable courts.

But they will bring more change at a faster rate—especially funding.

The key to rapid development in sub-Saharan Africa is digitalization. It's digitalization that can spread learning even to children with limited access to schools. It's digitalization that can help medical professionals see who has received vaccinations and track outbreaks of diseases. It's digitalization that can ensure that people who are eligible for government support receive that support. It's digitalization that will bring sub-Saharan Africa the transparency that people need to be able to trust governments and institutions.

But bringing that digitalization requires capital. It requires investors to make high risk bets on high risk technology ideas in a high risk environment. But high risks bring high rewards, and in sub-Saharan Africa, the reward is the kind of growth that has already transformed China and can do the same for much of Africa. In DFIs, the world has the tool it needs to deliver those funds that the private sector can't currently supply. Development funds need to step up, change their strategy, and start to act like venture capitalists in Africa—a continent that needs innovation. It will have a greater impact by creating trust, transparency, efficiency and growth that can lead to a sustainable development of sub-Saharan Africa.

Printed in Great Britain
by Amazon